Critical Realism, Post-positivism and the Possibility of Knowledge

D0551629

In this innovative approach to the problem of relativism, Ruth Groff argues that a critical realist approach to the concept of causality allows for a compelling response to the idea that all claims about the world are equally valid. Relativism, Groff observes, presupposes that the world is all possible ways – that it has no determinate, intrinsic features. The neo-Aristotelian view of causality advanced by critical realists (viz., that causality is a matter of the real powers that things have, in virtue of what they are, to affect other things in specific ways) represents a powerful challenge to the anti-realism that is at the heart of contemporary relativism.

Groff defends "realism about causality" through close discussions of Kant, Hilary Putnam, Brian Ellis and Charles Taylor, among others. In so doing she affirms critical realism, but with several important qualifications. In particular, she rejects the theory of truth advanced by Roy Bhaskar. She also attempts to both clarify and correct earlier critical realist attempts to apply realism about causality to the social sciences.

By connecting issues in metaphysics and philosophy of science to the problem of relativism, Groff bridges the gap between the philosophical literature and broader debates surrounding socio-political theory and postmodern and poststructuralist thought. This unique approach will make the book of interest to philosophers and socio-political theorists alike.

Ruth Groff is a Visiting Assistant Professor at Marquette University in Milwaukee, Wisconsin. She is interested in the history of Western social, political and moral thought and in theories about causality and the concept of truth. Past publications include "The Truth of the Matter," a systematic critique of Roy Bhaskar's theory of truth.

Routledge Studies in Critical Realism
Edited by Margaret Archer, Roy Bhaskar,
Andrew Collier, Tony Lawson and Alan Norrie

Critical realism is one of the most influential new developments in the philosophy of science and in the social sciences, providing a powerful alternative to positivism and post modernism. This series will explore the critical realist position in philosophy and across the social sciences.

Also published by Routledge:

Critical Realism: Interventions
Edited by Margaret Archer, Roy Bhaskar, Andrew Collier, Tony Lawson and Alan Norrie

Critical Realism
Essential readings
Edited by Margaret Archer, Roy Bhaskar, Andrew Collier, Tony Lawson and Alan Norrie

The Possibility of Naturalism Third Edition
A philosophical critique of the contemporary human sciences
Roy Bhaskar

Being and Worth
Andrew Collier

Quantum Theory and the Flight from Realism
Philosophical responses to quantum mechanics
Christopher Norris

From East to West
Odyssey of a soul
Roy Bhaskar

Realism and Racism
Concepts of race in sociological research
Bob Carter

Rational Choice Theory
Resisting colonisation
Edited by Margaret Archer and Jonathan Q. Tritter

Explaining Society
Critical realism in the social sciences
Berth Danermark, Mats Ekström, Jan Ch. Karlsson and Liselotte Jakobsen

Critical Realism, Post-positivism and the Possibility of Knowledge

Ruth Groff

Routledge
Taylor & Francis Group

LONDON AND NEW YORK

First published 2004
by Routledge
2 Park Square, Milton Park, Abingdon, Oxon, OX14 4RN

Simultaneously published in the USA and Canada
by Routledge
270 Madison Ave, New York NY 10016

Routledge is an imprint of the Taylor & Francis Group

Transferred to Digital Printing 2008

© 2004 Ruth Groff

Typeset in Sabon by Exe Valley Dataset Ltd, Exeter

British Library Cataloguing in Publication Data
A catalogue record for this book is available from the British Library

Library of Congress Cataloging in Publication Data
A catalog record for this book has been requested

ISBN10: 0–415–33473–X (hbk)
ISBN10: 0–415–46435–8 (pbk)

ISBN13: 978–0–415–33473–0 (hbk)
ISBN13: 978–0–415–46435–2 (pbk)

For my family

In memory of Jules Splaver (1906–2000) and
Marion Kepler Groff (1910–2002)

Contents

Acknowledgments

My impulse is to start by thanking my mom for teaching me the alphabet, and to then move forward from there. I will settle for beginning with Doug Bennett and Ken Sharpe, who first taught me to think philosophically, and Richard Schuldenfrei, who introduced me to the range of problems associated with positivism.

I have been guided and encouraged at every stage of this work by Asher Horowitz, David McNally and Rob Albritton. I can't even begin to count the hours of time that they have given to me, or the ways in which they have been supportive of me. A number of other people were generous enough to read drafts of chapters and discuss issues with me in their areas of expertise. Foremost amongst this group is Hugh Lacey, who first assigned *A Realist Theory of Science* to me when I was an undergraduate at Swarthmore College. Doug Porpora has also been a great help to me. I would also like to thank Jagdish Hattiangadi, Charles Chastain and Howard Engelskirchen.

As if this were not enough, I have had the invaluable benefit of being a participant of the Bhaskar listserv for the last six years. I cannot imagine how I could have written this book without the intellectual support and stimulation of the members of this unique virtual community. I would like to thank the list as a whole, and to especially thank Tobin Nellhaus, Colin Wight, Lewis Irwin, Mervyn Hartwig, Ronny Myhre (who introduced us to Brian Ellis and Irving Copi) and, again, Howard Engelskirchen and Doug Porpora.

I am lucky to have friends and family who always trusted that I would complete this project. I want to thank Juliet Sternberg (who even saw fit to send a magic wand), Steve Bross (and his family), Jonathan Sher and Janet Finegar, Victoria Littman, Sheryl Nestel, Kate Collins, Sheila Simpkins, Reese Simpkins, Sabine Neidhardt, Miriam Ticoll, Marlene Quesenberry, George Comninel and Leo Panitch. I want to thank Diane and Gary Laison, Helen Splaver, Janet Jackel, Betsy Eggerling and my entire wonderful, extended family, who encouraged me, reassured me, sent goodies, listened to drafts of chapters read over the phone and told me that they loved me.

Finally, I want to express my deepest gratitude to my parents, Jim and Meg Groff, to Noah Efron, who has been an unfailingly enthusiastic booster for over twenty years now, and to my sweetheart, David Lomax. I couldn't possibly put into a sentence or two what it has meant and continues to mean to me to enjoy David's love, intelligence, companionship, patience and good cheer. David always had faith in my abilities. I'm so happy to be able to share the publication of this book with him.

Thank you to Sage Publications for permission to reprint large portions of Chapter 4, which appeared in very close to its present form in *Philosophy of the Social Sciences* (30:3), and to Pearson Education Limited for permission to include Table 0.1 from *A Realist Theory of Science*.

1 Introduction
Relativism, anti-realism and causality

The problem at the heart of this book is the recent resurgence of relativism. In the wake of the well-deserved breakdown of positivism, it no longer seems possible to rationally assess competing knowledge claims. In the social sciences in particular, the fashionable post-positivist view is that any belief can be valid, depending upon one's perspective; that truth is simply a term of praise (or, alternately, a display of power); and that there is in fact no such thing as a reality that does not belong in quotation marks.

Relativism is problematic for a number of reasons, not the least of which is its political implications. If all beliefs about the world are equally valid, then no claims may be challenged on cognitive, or epistemic, grounds. At best, relativism can therefore be expected to discourage critical analysis and exchange – for what is the point of attempts to persuade through argumentation, if all claims about the world are by definition equally valid? At worst, it implies that critical exchange ought to be abandoned in favor of the use of force and/or non-rational charismatic appeals. In saying this I do not mean to paint a rosy picture of politics as consisting merely – or even essentially – of rational exchange between well-meaning public servants. It is worth responding to relativism not because ill-informed political leaders need only be enlightened, but because the widespread acceptance of false ideas plays a role in the perpetuation of unjust social relations.

In the following chapters I shall defend the merits of a position called critical realism. I believe that critical realism offers us a way out of the current morass. Specifically, critical realism allows us to cast off the anti-realism about causality that has dominated Western philosophy since Hume, and to replace it with a viable, realist alternative. Realism about the causal relation prohibits relativism on ontological grounds. If the relationship between causes and their effects is one of natural necessity, then, regardless of one's perspective – and notwithstanding the limits of our knowledge – it cannot be the case that all claims about the world are equally valid.

Critical realism is not an *epistemic* counter to relativism. It does not include a satisfactory account of the concept of truth or of justification. However, by predisposing us to distinguish between knowledge claims, which are socially produced and provisional in nature, and the concept of truth, which, in my view, is a transcendental condition of possibility of inquiry itself, it points us in the right direction in this area as well.

Two potential questions arise from this brief sketch. The first question has to do with method. If relativism has political consequences, why does it require a philosophical rather than an empirical response? The second question has to do with the focus on metaphysics. Why, if one were worried about relativism, would one choose to focus one's attention on a theory such as critical realism, which is primarily an account of causality? The answer to the first question is that relativism about knowledge claims is not just pernicious, but false. An empirical study of the effects of relativism on political culture could, and I believe would, help to demonstrate the former – that relativism undermines the possibility of rational critique, and is therefore antithetical to a just society. Such a study would not, however – and could not – show that relativism is false. Indeed, if one were to handle the matter empirically, one would have to take great care not to implicitly *endorse* the relativist position, by suggesting that it is false precisely *because* it is pernicious. It is in the very nature of the case, then, that relativism must be addressed philosophically if one is to challenge it on cognitive grounds.

But why should the concept of causality figure so prominently in such a response? What bearing does metaphysics in particular have on issues of justification and truth? The answer to this second question is that relativism presupposes anti-realism. In order for the claim that all knowledge claims are equally valid to itself be true, the world must be such that it can be described in all possible ways.[1] The view that this is so, that the world has no intrinsic structure, and that it can therefore be described in all possible ways, is the implicit ontology of contemporary relativism.

Realism about causality turns out to be the most interesting way to counter such a position. As we shall see, proponents of what could be called a dispositional theory of causality hold that the relationship between cause and effect is best understood neither as a subjective expectation, as Hume thought, nor as a Category of the

---

1 This holds even if one does not subscribe to a correspondence theory of truth. It is certainly consistent with both a coherence and a deflationary approach. And even proponents of epistemic or consensus theories of truth believe that warranted claims tell us something reliable about the world.

Understanding, as Kant believed, but rather as a real feature of the external world, grounded in the nature of the entities and processes to which it refers.[2] Such an approach presupposes that the world has a structure of its own – that it is comprised of natural kinds, which do what they do in virtue of what they are, or perhaps are what they are in virtue of what they do.[3] If this view of causality is correct, then relativism may be ruled out on ontological grounds. Of course, ruling out relativism on ontological grounds is no substitute for a theory of truth, or of justification. However it is a significant move, as I shall try to show.

The discussion to come is framed by these connections between politics and philosophy and between epistemology and metaphysics. In the end, my objective is to advance critical realism as an alternative to the relativism and attendant anti-realism that have come to characterize the post-positivist intellectual milieu. The main purpose of the present chapter is to provide a context for such an undertaking. I shall begin, therefore, by describing in more detail the conceptual development that worries me. I shall then turn to critical realism itself, setting out the basic rudiments of the position. Finally, I shall say a word about the kind of intervention that I want to make, and about what I do and do not hope to accomplish by it.

Post-positivist perspectivism

The phenomenon that concerns me is not reducible to the views of any one philosopher. While there are those whose thinking illustrates and/or has contributed to it, the phenomenon itself – which I shall call "post-positivist perspectivism" – is an overarching problematic, cutting across the social sciences and humanities. Emerging out of the breakdown of positivism, the problematic has to do with the limitations of our knowledge and of our thinking *about* knowledge.

---

2 Brian Ellis espouses a theory that is similar to critical realism in many respects; he refers to the ontological core of his position as "dispositional realism." The formulation above is mine rather than Ellis's, but it is influenced by Ellis's work. See Brian Ellis, *Scientific Essentialism*, Cambridge: Cambridge University Press, 2001.

3 There are disagreements amongst philosophers who write on these issues regarding whether things do what they do because of what they are, or are what they are because of what they can do. I have tried to describe the position in a way that would be acceptable to both sides in this debate. For a useful discussion see Anjan Chakravartty, "The Dispositional Essentialist View of Properties and Laws," forthcoming in *Philosophical Studies*, December 2003.

More specifically, it involves the repudiation of the concept of truth as a universal norm, and a deep suspicion of ontological realism. Prominent figures who hold such views range from Rorty and Putnam to Foucault, Lyotard and Flax, from Kuhn and Feyerabend to Derrida. Notably, most of the thinkers I've mentioned do not believe themselves to be either relativists or idealists. Nonetheless, especially as their ideas have filtered through the academy and into segments of the culture at large, they have contributed to a growing consensus that the concept of truth tells us little more than that a given person or group of people for some non-cognitive reason prefers to believe that x. As I have said, I regard this situation to be significant politically.

Jane Flax's piece "The End of Innocence" is an emblematic expression of the stance in question.[4] Flax's view is that the concepts of truth and reality have no genuine denotative meaning. They are simply words that philosophers (and others) use in order to impose their wills on others. By using such terms, Flax says, people are able to make it seem as though they are pursuing an objective dictate – an "innocent truth" – when in fact what they are trying to do is to advance their interests. So-called "truth," she says, is an effect of discourse. Each discourse has its own rules about what constitutes a meaningful statement and about how to determine the truth-value of given claims. "There is no way to test whether one story is closer to the truth than another," she says, "because there is no transcendental standpoint or mind unenmeshed in its own language and story."[5] What settles disputes is "prior agreement on rules, not the compelling power of objective truth."[6] In sum, "(a)ll knowledge is fictive and non-representational. As a product of the human mind, knowledge has no necessary relation to Truth or the Real."[7] Accordingly,

> (w)e should take responsibility for our desire . . . : what we really want is power in the world, not an innocent truth . . . Part of the purpose of claiming truth seems to be to compel agreement with our claim . . . We are often seeking a change in behavior or a win

---

4 This paragraph is a modified version of a passage that appeared in Ruth Groff, "Reason Reconsidered: Political Education, Critical Theory and the Concept of Rational Critique", unpublished Master of Arts thesis, University of Toronto, 1994. The article in question is Jane Flax, "The End of Innocence," in Judith Butler and Joan W. Scott (eds), *Feminists Theorize the Political*, London: Routledge, 1992.

5 Flax, "The End of Innocence," p. 454.

6 Ibid.

7 Ibid., p. 458.

for our side. If so, there may be more effective ways to attain agreement or produce change than to argue about truth.[8]

The presumed unity, stability and permanence of "reality," similarly, is an illusion created by Western philosophers, who have super-imposed binary oppositions onto the actual "flux and heterogeneity of the human and physical worlds."[9]

A more nuanced version is put forward by Richard Rorty.[10] Rorty would have it that he has successfully opted out of debates over the concept of truth and the nature of reality. Citing Dewey, he holds that the very questions of whether or not our accepted beliefs are "really" true and of whether or not the things that we encounter "really" exist are entirely meaningless. They can only arise, he says, if one has already adopted a way of looking at the world in which there is reason to think that we are fundamentally detached from, and unable to connect with, our environment. As answers to questions that make no sense to ask, the epistemological and ontological positions taken by traditional philosophical disputants simply take us further afield. If we are absolutely determined to try to fix the value of our beliefs, Rorty says, we should ask not whether or not they correspond to something non-human, but whether or not they promote social solidarity.

Rorty says that he cannot be charged with being a relativist because relativism, he says, is a theory of truth, and, as a pragmatist, he "does not have a theory of truth, much less a relativistic one."[11] There is a sense in which Rorty is right about this, though I don't think that he is right about why. To the extent that Rorty is a non-relativist, it is because he thinks that some beliefs – namely, "ours," as he puts it – are better than others.[12] As he says, "pragmatists should be ethnocentrists rather than relativists."[13] However, this only gets him so far. While Rorty thinks that "our" beliefs are better, he does not think that they tell us anything more about "reality" than

---

8 Ibid.
9 Ibid.
10 The following summary of Rorty's position is drawn largely though not exclusively from Richard Rorty, *Objectivity, Relativism and Truth: Philosophical Papers*, volume 1, Cambridge: Cambridge University Press, 1991 and Richard Rorty, *Philosophy and Social Hope*, London: Penguin Books, 1999.
11 Rorty, *Objectivity, Relativism and Truth*, p. 24.
12 Ibid., p. 29 and p. 38.
13 Richard Rorty, "Hilary Putnam and the Relativist Menace," in *Truth and Progress: Philosophical Papers*, vol. 3, New York: Cambridge University Press, 1998, p. 52.

do other beliefs. Our beliefs are better, but they are not better on epistemic grounds. They are better because they are the sorts of beliefs that people in societies with institutions such as ours are likely to have – which is to say (adding in the missing premise that our institutions are better) they are better on moral grounds. Rorty, of course, would reject the distinction that I have made between epistemic and moral justification. Nonetheless, it is important to be clear about what he does and does not mean when he says that some beliefs may be judged to be superior to others.

Meanwhile, Rorty does have a theory of truth. The concept of truth, he tells us, functions as "a general term of commendation."[14] It does not describe a relationship between propositions (or statements, sentences or words, if one prefers) and that to which they refer. It is simply an accolade. Rorty may be uninterested in pursuing the conversation further, but I don't see that this renders his a non-theory. What is in fact striking about Rorty's theory of truth is the resemblance that it bears to emotivist theories of moral discourse. From the perspective of emotivism, moral claims are expressions of approval or disapproval on the part of a speaker – combined, in the view of some emotivists, with an injunction to others to agree with the speaker. Thus, as C. L. Stevenson argued, "x is morally good" means "I approve of x. Do so as well."[15] Rorty's position is that epistemic discourse is equally self-referential: to say that a proposition is true is to say that one approves of it, and that others ought to do so as well.

Rorty also has an ontology, although admittedly he is careful to say that it doesn't tell us anything about what reality is "actually" like; it is just a belief that is useful to hold if one has certain objectives. "The pragmatist," he says,

> [differentiates] himself from the idealist. He agrees that there is such a thing as brute physical resistance – the pressure of light waves on Galileo's eyeball, or of the stone on Dr. Johnson's boot.[16]

However, he continues, such resistance is compatible with multiple, if not all possible, ways of describing it. This is because whatever it is

---

14 Rorty, *Objectivity, Relativism and Truth*, p. 23.
15 C. L. Stevenson, *Ethics and Language*, 1945, Ch. 2, cited in Alasdair MacIntyre, *After Virtue: A Study in Moral Theory*, Notre Dame, IN: University of Notre Dame Press, 1981, p. 12.
16 Rorty, *Objectivity, Relativism and Truth*, p. 81.

that exists has no internal characteristics – at least, not if one chooses to look at things in this way. Those things that we count as real are like numbers, Rorty says, "which are an admirable example of something which it is difficult to describe in essentialist language."[17] Rorty points to the number 17. Seventeen cannot be described except in terms of its relationships to other numbers – there is no "intrinsic seventeenness of 17," as he puts it.[18] "We anti-essentialists," Rorty writes,

> . . . suggest that you think of all such objects as resembling numbers in the following respect: there is nothing to be known about them except an initially large, and forever expandable, web of relations to other objects.[19]

Rorty connects the idea that "there are, so to speak, relations all the way down, all the way up, and all the way out in every direction" to psychological nominalism.[20] "For psychological nominalists," he says,

> no description of an object is more a description of the "real", as opposed to the "apparent", object than any other, nor are any of them descriptions of, so to speak, the object's relation to itself – of its identity with its own essence.[21]

Thus, he writes, "as many facts are brought into the world as there are languages for describing [a] causal transaction."[22] Any reference to "unmediated causal forces," he concludes, is "pointless."[23]

It is worth noting that for both Flax and Rorty a correspondence approach to the concept of truth and a commitment to ontological realism are positions that proponents take for large-scale ethical and/or religious reasons. The directive from both is that we grow up, and be done with the need for philosophically grounded moral certitude. While I am sympathetic to such an account, I want to challenge it as a way of framing the issues at hand. A passing glance at the history of philosophy shows that a correspondence approach to truth, ontological realism and moral absolutism do not always line up in a given thinker's work. Aristotle, for example, was a proponent

---

17 Rorty, *Philosophy and Social Hope*, p. 52.
18 Ibid., p. 53.
19 Ibid.
20 Ibid., pp. 53–54.
21 Ibid., p. 54.
22 Rorty, *Objectivity, Relativism and Truth*, p. 81.
23 Ibid.

of the first two positions but not of the third. Kant is ambiguous on the first, opposed to what he calls "transcendental" versions of the second and in strong support of the third. The paradigmatic logical positivist A. J. Ayer, who thought that scientific knowledge claims could be mapped onto purely empirical sense-data, held that moral claims were literally meaningless.

Rorty might be expected to reply that where we see a commitment to the concepts of truth and reality on the one hand, combined with moral heterodoxy on the other, we have simply found the conditions that lead religious needs to be displaced onto epistemology and metaphysics. Precisely insofar as our moral views no longer seem to be objectively anchored, we turn to scientific "facts" to tell us our place in the universe. As for the Aristotelian case, he might say, there is a definite and knowable Good for human beings within Aristotle's philosophy, even if particular moral judgments can only be as sure as their object permits. And Kant would have it that we make contact with a noumenal realm via practical reason.

In fact Rorty may be right, in the end, to think that the history of Western philosophy is one of religious desire – or, as he would put it, to say that the story can be told that way to productive effect. Even so, it doesn't follow that moral certitude is the only relevant variable in the present discussion. My own concern, for example, is not with the ambiguity of ethical norms. What I care about is our capacity to challenge political-economic knowledge claims on epistemic grounds. I believe that even if we renounce all appeal to moral absolutes, we still need to be able to critically assess the front-page news. While it is important to ask whose interests are served by a given presentation of events, it is also important to be able to ask whether or not an alleged event actually occurred. The whole notion of ideology critique has for so long been associated with the defense of a full-blown and often dogmatically held "grand narrative," to use Lyotard's term, that there is a tendency to discount the very real problem of falsehood. From my perspective, then, the stakes are less grandiose than Flax and Rorty would have it, but they are still very high. The problem with post-positivist perspectivism is not that it leaves us on our own to work out for ourselves what to believe about the world. The problem is that it leaves us without any way to talk seriously about deception and error.

As I said at the outset, my intention is to both assess and defend an alternative to post-positivist perspectivism – an alternative that I believe represents a more complete break with positivism than do the various post-positivist positions on offer. The approach that I want to consider is called critical realism. In the chapters to come I shall be concerned to see whether or not, and if so to what extent and in what manner, critical realism allows us to meet the challenges of relativism and anti-realism posed by post-positivism. Since I do not subscribe to the view that theory choice – even between philosophical accounts – is a non-cognitive process, I cannot simply announce my positive feeling about critical realism, and enjoin others to share the sentiment. Instead I will have to try to show that the approach that I support is compelling on cognitive grounds. Let me begin with an overview of the position itself.

Critical realism

> The first time a man saw the communication of motion by impulse, as by the shock of two billiard balls, he could not pronounce that the one event was connected, but only that it was conjoined with the other. After he has observed several instances of this nature, he then pronounces them to be connected. What alteration has happened to give rise to this new idea of connection? Nothing but that he now feels these events to be connected in his imagination, and can readily foretell the existence of one from the appearance of the other.
>
> (David Hume)[24]

> When we think of causality and action we look to such images as a springtime plant forcing its way upwards towards the light, as the pulsing, surging movement of the protoplasm within an amoeba, of a flash of radiation as a positron and an electron meet, of the enormous flux of electromagnetic radiation from a star, of the mobility and imaginative control of his own actions exercised by a human being, of the potent configuration of a magnetic field. For us, a billiard table is relevant to philosophy only in so far as it is conceived of as surrounded by the players, and embedded within a gravitational field.
>
> (Rom Harré and E. H. Madden)[25]

> The principle of causation remains a wishful conviction.
>
> (M. J. Garcia-Encinas)[26]

24 David Hume, *An Inquiry Concerning Human Understanding*, in *On Human Nature and the Understanding* (ed. Antony Flew), New York: Collier Books, 1962, p. 88.

25 R. Harré and E. H. Madden, *Causal Powers: A Theory of Natural Necessity*, Totowa, NJ: Rowman and Littlefield, 1975, p. 7.

26 M. J. Garcia-Encinas, "Sullivan on the Principle that Everything Has a Cause," in *Dialogue: Canadian Philosophical Review*, XLI(3), Summer 2002, p. 435.

The term critical realism is associated with the earlier work of Roy Bhaskar. Bhaskar's first book, entitled *A Realist Theory of Science* (hereafter *RTS*), was published in 1975.[27] In it he defended a position that he called transcendental realism. *RTS* was followed in 1979 by *The Possibility of Naturalism* (hereafter *PON*).[28] In *PON*, Bhaskar argued for an extension of transcendental realism to the social sciences. The stance that he took there he dubbed critical naturalism. Readers then combined the two terms, producing the name critical realism. With the publication of *Dialectic: The Pulse of Freedom* in 1993,[29] critical realism was transformed into what Bhaskar then called dialectical critical realism. By 2000, Bhaskar began to refer to his position as transcendental dialectical critical realism. Recently he has adopted the phrase "philosophy of meta-reality" to characterize the latest developments in his thinking. I am interested in Bhaskar's early work – which is to say critical realism – and also in his theory of truth, which is contained in *Dialectic: The Pulse of Freedom* and *Plato, Etc.*[30] When I am referring to Bhaskar's early position as a whole, I shall use the term critical realism. When I am talking specifically about the core claims of either *RTS* or *PON*, I shall use the terms transcendental realism and critical naturalism respectively.

Critical realism can be attached to three theses: ontological realism, epistemological relativism and judgmental rationality.[31] In Bhaskar's hands, ontological realism is the general view (a) that there are processes in the natural world that occur (and entities that exist) independently of human intervention, and (b) that the social world is neither voluntaristically produced by, nor reducible to, the thoughts or actions of individuals. With respect to natural and social phenomena alike, Bhaskar's realism is linked to the concept of ontological stratification, or depth. Reality is said to be stratified in the sense that manifest events are seen as being the effects of underlying causal mechanisms. Causal mechanisms are conceived as entities[32] that have

27 Roy Bhaskar, *A Realist Theory of Science*, Sussex: The Harvester Press Limited, 1978 (first published 1975).

28 Roy Bhaskar, *The Possibility of Naturalism: A Philosophical Critique of the Contemporary Human Sciences*, 3rd edition, London: Routledge, 1998, first published in 1979 by The Harvester Press.

29 Roy Bhaskar, *Dialectic: The Pulse of Freedom*, London: Verso, 1993.

30 Roy Bhaskar, *Plato, Etc.: The Problems of Philosophy and their Solution*, London: Verso, 1994.

31 Roy Bhaskar, *Scientific Realism and Human Emancipation*, London: Verso, 1986, p. 24.

32 In *PON* Bhaskar claims that relationships and reasons alike, and not just entities, are causally efficacious. As I argue in Chapter 5, I believe that Bhaskar here shifts from talking about efficient cause to talking about formal and final cause.

the power to effect change (or sometimes simply as being such powers). Further, they are thought to bear (or be) such powers essentially. Both the powers and the entities that bear them are held to be real, in virtue of being potentially – even when not actually – causally efficacious, but not necessarily to be empirically accessible. Reality, from this perspective, is regarded as being of (as yet) indeterminate depth: any given causal mechanism itself is assumed to itself be the product of an underlying causal process.

These are fairly sweeping claims, though Bhaskar does put forward arguments in their support. I shall do my best to reconstruct Bhaskar's reasoning, but before doing so let me note that there are a number of different things that he would have us accept as real. Specifically, Bhaskar can be seen to be advancing realism about (1) entities of various sorts, (2) processes of certain sorts, namely, causal ones, (3) powers, by which Bhaskar means capacities for behavior of certain sorts, and (4) causality itself. (In *PON*, social relations and reasons are added to the list.) I think that Bhaskar is perhaps not careful enough in differentiating between these assertions. Nonetheless, outside of a small circle of professional metaphysicians and philosophers of science, debates over realism tend to be about entities. It is one of the valuable features of critical realism, in my view, that it ultimately shifts the ontological focus away from entities and onto processes, powers and causality itself.

The linchpin of Bhaskar's argument for ontological realism in relation to the natural world is an argument concerning experimentation. Experiments, Bhaskar says, are at odds with the dominant conception of what a causal law is – and, by extension, with the dominant philosophical conception of what causality is. The widely accepted understanding of causal laws is fundamentally Humean: a causal law is a general statement based on the perceived constant conjunction of two events. Causality itself, meanwhile, is nothing other than an expectation that such regularities will persist over time. From this perspective, the laws of nature are fundamentally contingent.[33] In principle, the "causal" relationships between phenomena could be entirely different than they are at present.[34] Kantians modify the Humean position by saying that the very fact that phenomena

---

33 My understanding of this aspect of the Humean account comes from Ellis, *Scientific Essentialism*. See especially, Chapters 1, 3, 6, 7 and 8.
34 The emphasis on contingency comes from Ellis. Bhaskar, by contrast, is more concerned to show that the only way that the approach is intelligible is if regularity determinism in the context of a closed system fills in, as it were, for a concept of natural necessity in open systems.

appear causally related at all is a necessary feature of our experience of them. But, as Bhaskar maintains – and as I shall argue in more detail in Chapter 2 – Kant did not break with Hume with respect to the idea that causal necessity does not inhere in the external world.

Bhaskar's claim is that the practice of natural scientific experimentation presupposes exactly what the Humean position denies: the existence of causal powers, conceived in naturalistic terms, which account for the relationship of causal necessity. Scientific experiments, Bhaskar reminds us, consist of the artificial generation of regularities. The idea is that by bringing about a particular constant conjunction of events in an artificial environment – one in which the number of causal variables is limited – we will find out something about what the world is like *outside* such an environment. This belief, however – that experiments can tell us something about what the world is like *outside* the experimental setting – presupposes that while scientists do (and in general must) actively induce regularities, they do not thereby produce the *causes* of such regularities.[35] If such a presupposition were not in place, and instead experimenters were thought to produce not just regular conjunctions but the laws governing such conjunctions, then such laws could not be expected to hold outside experimental settings. To quote Bhaskar, "just because the experimenter is a causal agent of the sequence of events, there must be an ontological distinction between the sequence he generates and the causal law it enables him to identify. Any other conclusion renders experimental activity pointless."[36] And again:

> [I]t lies within the power of every reasonably intelligent schoolboy or moderately clumsy research worker to upset the results of even the best designed experiment, but we do not thereby suppose they have the power to overturn the laws of nature. I can quite easily affect any sequence of events designed to test say Coulomb's or Guy-Lussac's law, but I have no more power over the relationship the laws describe than the men who discovered them had.[37]

The argument, then, is that if experiments are what we think they are, then it must be that causal laws refer to something other than regularities.

A proponent of the view that laws refer to regularities might be expected to object that Bhaskar has misconceived the nature of

35 Thanks to Hugh Lacey for helping to clarify my understanding of this point.
36 Bhaskar, *RTS*, p. 54.
37 Ibid., p. 34.

experiments. Experimenters do not induce regularities, he or she would say. Rather, they simply create environments in which those regularities that occur naturally can be observed without the distraction of irrelevant variables. There is no problem in explaining how the results of experiments can be generalized, because in a real sense there is nothing to be generalized: regularities do exist outside experimental settings; we just can't see them clearly. The response to this is that it is not, in fact, a difficult matter to determine whether or not scientifically significant regularities occur spontaneously in non-artificial environments. Patently, they don't – which is why experiments are required.[38]

The attempt to protect the thesis of regularity determinism, as Bhaskar calls it, leads its proponents toward either or both of two regresses, he says. Either they have to say that the system in question does not take in enough variables, or they have to say that the components of the system have not been described in basic (i.e., atomistic) enough terms. In the former case, "a full causal statement would seem to entail a complete state-description (or a complete history) of the world."[39] In the latter case, "a causal statement entails a complete reduction of things into their presumed atomistic components (or their original conditions)."[40] Neither of these alternatives is satisfactory, Bhaskar contends. Moreover, neither allows us to make statements of the sort: "Event B did not follow event A because thing x did not exercise its power to cause B."[41] There is, however, no need for us to defend at all costs a theory of causal laws that requires a dogmatic commitment to the idea that the natural world is a closed system. Instead, says Bhaskar, we can conceive of causal laws as referring to the powers that entities have (and sometimes just are) to bring about precisely those patterns of events that can be observed in experimental settings. Unlike regularities, the presence of dispositional capacities does not presuppose that the operational context is a closed system.

Bhaskar's concept of a generative mechanism is very close to that of Rom Harré (1975), whose book *Causal Powers: A Theory of Natural Necessity* (co-written with E. H. Madden) appeared in print in the same year as *RTS*, and whose work Bhaskar acknowledges as

---

38 Thanks to Hugh Lacey for this point.
39 Bhaskar, *RTS*, p. 77.
40 Ibid.
41 As Bhaskar puts it, the regularity determinist "cannot allow that there is a sense to a statement about what an individual can do independently of whether or not it will do it." Bhaskar, *RTS*, p. 78.

having significantly influenced his thinking in *RTS*.[42] Harré and Madden defended a realist approach to causality in which causal relationships were seen to be a matter of "powerful particulars" behaving as they must, given what they they are.[43] Their position was that the world is made up of "causally potent thing[s]"[44] – "forceful objects"[45] that act as causal agents in that their behavior effects change in other objects. How an object will behave under given conditions, they said, is determined by what it is, i.e., by those properties that it holds essentially. It follows from this that an object cannot act in a manner that is at *odds* with what it is. The position that they were defending, Harré and Madden noted, involves the concept of natural kinds. It also involves a recovery of the notion of real as opposed to nominal essences. Harré and Madden argued that there is nothing unscientific or occult about such an ontology. While the metaphysics is radically anti-Humean (and at base non-Cartesian), there is no suggestion that objects are fulfilling inner purposes or, except in the case of sentient creatures, acting intentionally. Nor is there any suggestion that knowledge of essential properties is to be gained in a mysterious or non-empirical way. Harré and Madden pointed to the atomic structure of copper as an example of a real essence.

In *RTS*, Bhaskar follows Harré and Madden in connecting generative mechanisms – and by extension causal laws and causality itself – to the behavior of entities.[46] For example, he writes "reference to causal laws involves centrally reference to *causal agents*; that is, to things endowed with causal powers."[47] And even more to the point: "only things and materials and people have 'powers.'"[48] There is, however, a discernible difference of emphasis between Bhaskar and Harré and Madden. Specifically, Bhaskar is more concerned with the *powers* of things than with things as such. Thus while for Harré and

---

42 Roy Bhaskar and Tony Lawson, "Introduction: Basic Texts and Developments," in Margaret Archer, Roy Bhaskar, Andrew Collier, Tony Lawson and Alan Norrie (eds), *Critical Realism: Essential Readings*, London: Routledge, 1998, p. 6.
43 R. Harré and E. H. Madden, *Causal Powers*, p. 5.
44 Ibid., p. 48.
45 Ibid., p. 57.
46 Harré and Madden argue that causality is not a "thing," and that to think of it as such is simply to reify the capacities of powerful particulars. "There are not both things and causality in nature, but causally active things," they write (Harré and Madden, *Causal Powers*, p. 57). My feeling is that it is legitimate to talk about causality as such, even if one defines it as the display of powers that are borne by a particular.
47 Bhaskar, *RTS*, p. 49.
48 Ibid., p. 78.

Madden it is the concept of a powerful particular that is central, for Bhaskar it is the concept of a power itself (and ultimately the concept of a tendency for a power to be expressed) that is the analytic focus. Bhaskar's position also differs from that of Harré and Madden in that Harré and Madden vigorously maintain that we in fact experience causal powers directly – in, for example, the feel of the wind or the heat of the flame.[49] Bhaskar seems to think that this is sometimes so,[50] but emphasizes both that causal powers exist whether they are perceived or not, and that perception of them is not a criterion of their existence. Like Harré and Madden, however, Bhaskar's view is that causal laws refer ultimately to the tendencies that things have to behave in certain ways – by which he means not that laws express the statistical likelihood of the occurrence of a pattern of events, but rather that they describe "potentialities which may be exercised or as it were 'in play' without being realized or manifest in any particular outcome."[51]

Bhaskar also agrees with Harré and Madden that things behave the way that they do because of what they are. As Harré and Madden observe, such a view commits one to the existence of natural kinds, as well as to the existence of real rather than nominal essences. As will be discussed in more detail in Chapter 3, the language of real and nominal essences comes from Locke. The term real essence refers to the internal, physical constitution of a thing. The term nominal essence, by contrast, refers to those manifest features of a thing that we regard as indispensable to our concept of it. Locke thought that we could not know the internal constitutions of things, and that therefore any sorting of objects into kinds is necessarily done on the basis of their nominal essences. For Bhaskar, as for Harré and Madden, there is no reason to think that we cannot gain fallible knowledge of the internal constitution of objects in our world – and even less reason to think that things do not have internal constitutions.

Bhaskar agrees with Harré and Madden that a thing cannot behave in a way that is *contrary* to its nature. A thing of one kind can change into a thing of another kind, but it cannot remain a thing of a given kind and yet behave in a way that is at odds with the essence of things of that kind. Harré and Madden express the point as follows:

> It is physically impossible for a substance to act or react incompatibly with its own nature. It is not impossible for an object or

49 Harré and Madden, *Causal Powers*, pp. 49–58.
50 See *RTS*, p. 90.
51 Bhaskar, *RTS*, p. 50.

sample to act and react differently at one time rather than other. But in general it *cannot* do so under the same circumambient conditions and be deemed to have remained the same substance. In short, the relation between what a thing is and what it is capable of doing and undergoing is naturally necessary.[52]

Bhaskar, similarly, writes:

a thing must tend to act the way it does if it is to be the kind of thing it is. If a thing is a stick of gelignite it must explode if certain conditions materialize. Since anything that did not explode in those circumstances would not be a stick of gelignite but some other substance.[53]

I don't know that such a claim adds anything to the concept of a natural kind, but it underscores the ontological distance between transcendental realism and the Humean metaphysic, as Brian Ellis, another proponent of this basic approach, has called it.[54] From the more familiar Humean perspective, there is nothing at all necessary about the way that things presently behave. As Ellis observes, the Humean view is that a thing's behavior is determined not by what it is, but rather by the patterns of regularity that obtain in the world. What those patterns happen to be is purely contingent, says the Humean (this because it is logically permissible to assume that a regularity that holds at present will no longer hold five minutes from now).[55] Thus it is entirely possible, from the Humean perspective, that something could act in a way that it has never acted before, i.e., in a way that is contrary to its purported "nature."

It may be useful at this stage to return to the group of ontological commitments that I identified at the outset. Critical realism, I said, involves realism about entities, processes, powers and, I want to say, causality itself. It also involves claims for the existence of natural kinds and of real essences, meaning that it involves the idea that the natural world has an intrinsic structure of its own, ontologically independent of our experience of it. Bhaskar expresses these commitments via two different sets of categories, upon which he relies fairly heavily, which we are now in a position to appreciate.

The first set of categories, related to the concept of ontological depth mentioned earlier, is the more elaborate of the two. It is a

52 Harré and Madden, *Causal Powers* p. 14.
53 Bhaskar, *RTS*, p. 214.
54 Ellis, *Scientific Essentialism*, p. 47.
55 Ibid., and *passim*.

matrix, comprised along one axis of the categories of "mechanisms," "events" and "experiences," and along the other of the categories of "the domain of the Real," "the domain of the Actual" and "the domain of the Empirical." The matrix is a way of expressing the idea that mechanisms do not always produce the events that they have the power to bring about, and that, of those events that do occur, not all are experienced by a subject. (Bhaskar depicts this symbolically as dr>da>de.[56])

Table 1

	Domain of real	Domain of actual	Domain of empirical
Mechanisms	•		
Events	•	•	
Experiences	•	•	•

© Copyright Roy Bhaskar, 1975, 1978, The Harvester Press Limited, reprinted by permission of Pearson Education Limited.

The broadly Humean approach to causality is flawed, Bhaskar maintains, because by identifying laws with observed regularities, its proponents equate the operation of causal mechanisms with the experience of regular sequences of events. Such an equation is problematic in several ways. It is questionable ontologically because it amounts to a collapse of the domains of the real and the actual into the domain of the empirical, such that it is only experiences of events (or, if we are feeling ontologically generous, events, though only those that have been experienced) that are thought to exist. It is questionable both epistemologically and sociologically because it obscures the "work" of experimental science, as Bhaskar puts it – which is precisely to create artificially closed settings in which mechanisms *do* produce constant conjunctions, which *are* indeed experienced by trained subjects – making it seem as though laws and "facts" exist ready-made, waiting to be read off from our experience of the world.

The second set of categories that Bhaskar introduces is that of the "intransitive" and "transitive objects of science." The intransitive object of science is defined as "the real things and structures, mechanisms and processes, events and possibilities of the world . . . [not] in any way dependent on our knowledge, let alone perception, of them."[57] It is "the unchanging real objects that exist outside of the

---

56 Bhaskar, *RTS*, p. 56.
57 Ibid., p. 22.

scientific process."[58] Or again, as Bhaskar puts it in the opening paragraph of *RTS*,

> knowledge is "*of*" things which are not produced by men at all: the specific gravity of mercury, the process of electrolysis, the mechanism of light propagation. None of these "objects of knowledge" depend upon human activity. If men ceased to exist, sound would continue to travel and heavy bodies fall to the earth in exactly the same way, though ex hypothesi there would be no-one to know it.[59]

The transitive object of science, by contrast, is defined as "the changing cognitive objects that are produced within science as a function of scientific practice."[60] It may be thought of as the accumulated intellectual resources, upon which and with which natural scientists work – analogous in this respect to Althusser's Generalities. Unlike the intransitive object, the transitive object of science is entirely conceptual in nature: "[k]nowledge of B is produced by means of knowledge of A, but both items of knowledge exist only in thought," Bhaskar writes.[61]

The relationship between the intransitive and transitive objects of science is often misconceived, according to Bhaskar. Two common errors are often made. The first Bhaskar calls the "epistemic fallacy"; the second he terms the "ontic fallacy." The epistemic fallacy is "the view that statements about being can be reduced to or analyzed in terms of statements about knowledge; i.e., that ontological questions can always be transposed into epistemological terms."[62] The ontic fallacy, meanwhile, is "the definition or assumption of the compulsive determination of knowledge by being."[63] Someone who commits the epistemic fallacy implicitly equates the intransitive and transitive objects of science by suggesting that statements about the former are equivalent to statements about the latter. Someone who commits the ontic fallacy collapses the transitive object of science into the intransitive object by suggesting that the former is directly given, or in some sense automatically generated, by the latter. As mistakes in reasoning,

---

58 Roy Bhaskar, *Reclaiming Reality: A Critical Introduction to Contemporary Philosophy*, London: Verso, 1989, p. 26.
59 Bhaskar, *RTS*, p. 21.
60 Bhaskar, *Reclaiming Reality*, p. 27.
61 Bhaskar, *RTS*, p. 23.
62 Ibid., p. 36.
63 Roy Bhaskar, *Plato, Etc.: The Problems of Philosophy and their Resolution*, London: Verso, 1994, p. 253.

both the epistemic and the ontic fallacies occur within the transitive dimension.

The category of the transitive object of science leads to the second basic thesis of critical realism, a principle that Bhaskar calls epistemological relativism. Bhaskar uses the terminology in a non-standard way. By epistemological relativism he means not that the truth-value of propositions is relative to a given speaker or audience, but rather that theories themselves are ontologically "relative" to human subjectivity in a way that causal mechanisms are not. Knowledge claims, he maintains, are socio-historical artifacts; they are produced rather than discovered, and they change over time. Bhaskar takes it that with the thesis of epistemological relativism he has avoided two possible mistakes. The first is the ontic fallacy – thinking that knowledge claims are simply given to us by the world. The second is to view knowledge as being constructed, but as being constructed spontaneously, without reference to existing beliefs and social conditions. Knowledge production, Bhaskar says, is best thought of not as a process of creation *ex nihilo*, but rather as a process whereby existing ideas are transformed into new ones.

Several different claims are associated with the thesis of epistemological relativism.[64] The first of these is that knowledge must be understood to be fallible. This is an important claim (though it is not unique to Bhaskar), as it runs counter to the idea that what we call knowledge is by definition both justified and true. Admittedly, I am perhaps inclined to make more of this point than might Bhaskar. As a proponent of the correspondence theory of truth, I distinguish between justification and truth. In saying that we are justified in *believing* a claim to be true, I believe that we are saying something other than that it is in *fact* true. Dropping "true" from the definition of knowledge as "justified, true belief" is therefore a significant step, in my view. Bhaskar, by contrast, endorses an epistemic, or consensus, theory of truth in *RTS*. For a consensus theorist, to say that a belief is true just *is* to say that we are justified in believing it to be true. There is in a sense no need, from such a perspective, to specify that knowledge is both justified *and* true. In either case, however, the implication of adopting a fallibilist view of knowledge is that there can be no difference in kind between knowledge and well-supported-beliefs-that-might-be-false. In his later work, Bhaskar proposes a theory of truth in which the concept is taken to designate real essences. As I

---

64 I don't believe that the claims in question are actually entailed by the thesis of epistemological relativism, although Bhaskar sometimes writes as though they are.

argue in Chapter 4, this move has the effect of weakening the commitment to fallibilism associated with the principle of epistemic relativism as Bhaskar construes it.

The second claim associated with the thesis of epistemological relativism is that scientific inquiry is an active process, and one that is inherently social. Knowledge production involves work of two different kinds, says Bhaskar. In the case of the natural sciences, it involves physical intervention in the world via experimentation (Bhaskar does not regard experimentation in the social sciences as being legitimately possible, and so does not discuss the type of intervention that this involves); in all cases, it involves the conceptual transformation of previously held ideas. Such a view of knowledge production has a bearing on how one thinks of regularities, how one thinks of facts and how one thinks of theories. Regularities are understood to be events that are brought about by researchers, in the context of an ongoing, highly institutionalized social practice. Facts, in turn, are defined as theoretically informed experiences of such events. Theories, finally, are held to be transformations of earlier theories, rather than snapshots of sense data. As already noted, Bhaskar argues that the positivist philosophy of science masks all of this labor. With respect to experiments, both the occurrence and the experience of artificially produced regularities are naturalized, such that – as we have seen – the world is thought to be a naturally closed system, and what are in reality highly mediated experiences are taken to be passive registrations of sensory input. (At the same time, there is what might be called a "de-naturalization" of causality itself.) With respect to the development of scientific explanations, meanwhile, theories are presumed to be statements of scientists' purportedly unmediated experience of the world.

Finally, epistemological relativism is associated with the view that scientists' descriptions of the world are always theoretically informed (a position that is implicit in the view that the cognitive task undertaken by scientists is to use concepts to produce other concepts). Unlike Hilary Putnam, for example, whose treatment of these issues I shall discuss at length in Chapter 3, Bhaskar draws no special ontological or epistemological conclusions from this idea. For Putnam, the fact that we know the world under some theoretical description means that we cannot have knowledge of the world "itself." Bhaskar agrees that our cognitive encounter with the world is mediated by concepts. From a critical realist perspective, however, this does not imply that we have no cognitive access to the world "itself" – let alone that the world itself has no form. Rather, it tells us only that the knowledge of the world that we *do* gain is inherently theoretical. That the whole notion of "sense-data" is indefensible tells us something important about the deficiencies of positivism, but it places neither ontological conditions on the world nor epistemic limits upon us.

The third thesis of critical realism is what Bhaskar refers to as rationality at the level of judgment. The claim here is that even though scientific knowledge is both fallible and socially grounded, the choice between competing scientific theories is nonetheless a rational one. That rational deliberation over rival theories is possible, Bhaskar says, is established by the very fact that they are rivals. Truly incommensurable theories or paradigms would in a real sense not be alternatives in the way that competing explanations in the history of science have been. Theory selection is rational in that scientists make reference to existing knowledge in their collective effort to determine the relative merits of a given approach. The fact that they cannot compare a theory to unmediated sensory experience does not mean that there is no way to assess its explanatory power, as Bhaskar puts it, or that scientific change is arbitrary and non-rational. As argued in Chapter 4, my own view is that the issues of justification and of the meaning of the concept of truth are not well theorized in Bhaskar's work. With respect to justification, the notion of explanatory power is a good one. However there is need for further elaboration. With respect to the concept of truth, I do not believe that it is possible for a realist to successfully side-step the correspondence theory.

Each of the theses identified here is explored in the chapters to come, though I pay more attention to the concepts of causality and truth than I do to the claim that knowledge is a social product and/or that facts are theory dependent. In Chapter 2, I focus almost entirely on the thesis of ontological realism. My aim there is to show that the conception of causality defended by Bhaskar and others presents a viable alternative to the anti-naturalist rejoinder to Hume put forward by Kant. In Chapter 3, meanwhile, I continue the discussion of causality begun in Chapter 2, and also consider the relationship between ontological realism and epistemological relativism. I pursue these issues through an analysis of Hilary Putnam's case for what he calls "internal realism." In Chapter 4, I consider Bhaskar's theory of truth. I argue there that the concept of "alethic truth," as he terms it, is a misnomer for the notion of a real essence, and that the identification of truth with being is not helpful. In Chapter 5, I return to the issue of ontological realism by considering Bhaskar's extension of transcendental realism to the social sciences and psychology. There I address the question of whether or not social structures may be regarded as being causal bearers, analogous to generative mechanisms in nature. I address the question via the work of Rom Harré and Charles Varela, and also (at greater length) through the work of

Brian Ellis, a fellow "scientific essentialist," as he puts it. Chapter 5 also contains a discussion of Bhaskar's conception of individual agency. Finally, I conclude in Chapter 6 by reflecting upon the significance of critical realism relative to the challenges posed by post-positivist perspectivism.

Rationale

As I've said, my objective is to defend an alternative to positivism that does not lead to the relativism and anti-realism characteristic of post-positivism. I have approached the task primarily by engaging with a set of interlocutors who cannot (or at least ought not) be easily dismissed by critical realists: Kant, Hilary Putnam, Brian Ellis, Charles Taylor. By employing such a strategy I may run the risk of appearing not to have subjected critical realism to rigorous enough of a test: why not choose Derrida, or Judith Butler, or even Rorty? In some ways, however, it is more difficult – and it is certainly at least as productive – to engage with those with whom there is some amount of common ground than with those with whom there is none. In any case, I have introduced into the conversation positions that I believe must be taken seriously. I should note that in Chapter 4 there is no outside interlocutor as there is in the other chapters. While I draw there upon work by William Alston, I treat Alston's position as a point of reference in characterizing my own views, rather than as a direct counter to an aspect of critical realism.

Roy Bhaskar is neither the first nor the only proponent of the kind of approach that interests me. Harré and Madden's *Causal Powers* and Brian Ellis's more recent *Scientific Essentialism* are equally compelling statements of the general position as *A Realist Theory of Science*. I have nonetheless chosen to focus on Bhaskar. I have done so for several reasons. The first is that Bhaskar is the only one of the three who applies his theory of causality to social structures. Harré holds that in the social realm it is only individual persons who have causal efficacy. For Ellis, meanwhile, the deciding factor is whether or not an entity falls into a natural kind that can be said to have an essence. Ellis is ambivalent about whether or not individuals meet this criterion, but is adamant that social structures do not. With slight amendment, I think that Bhaskar's position is defensible. The second reason for which I have focused on Bhaskar is that, of the three, he has had the widest appeal. While he is perhaps less well known than the others in professional philosophical circles, he has a broader following across the social sciences – and even into the humanities – than does either Harré or Ellis. There is now an International Association for Critical Realism, an annual, international conference on critical realism and an academic *Journal of Critical Realism*. Third – and this is a point related to the previous two – Bhaskar has more of a connection to the field of political economy than do the others. He argues, for example, that critical realism is the implicit philosophy of science of Marx's analysis in *Capital*. While this is not a thread that I explore in this book, it contributes to my sense that Bhaskar's work represents a potential point of entry into epistemology and metaphysics for practicing social scientists. Finally, Bhaskar is interesting because he explicitly connects critical realism to the project of human emancipation. Successful struggles for social justice, he suggests, require that we be able to identify those structures that arrest our capabilities. The core ideological function of positivism in the social sciences, he argues, is precisely to render such underlying mechanisms invisible.[65] This type of attention to the political function of philosophical ideas is an invaluable dimension of Bhaskar's thinking in my view.

Finally, before moving on let me say that while I believe that critical realism can help us to move beyond post-positivism, I do not regard it as philosophical panacea. For one thing, I heartily disagree with Bhaskar's theory of truth. I also suspect that the theory of language contained in Bhaskar's later work is unsatisfactory. Beyond considerations such as these, however, there is simply the matter of philosophical temper. I am not inclined to see the work of any one thinker as being entirely sufficient, or worthy of ultimate allegiance or adulation. This is not to repeat the platitude that "there is something of value in every position," for I do not believe that this is so. Rather it is an attempt to resist dogmatism. My thesis, then, is fairly modest: realism about causality, in conjunction with a recognition of the social character of knowledge and the retention of the norm of correspondence as a transcendental condition of possibility of inquiry, provides a much-needed set of stepping stones out of the post-positivist quagmire in which we presently find ourselves.

---

65 Bhaskar, *Reclaiming Reality*, p. 9 and *passim*.

2 On the necessity of necessary connections

Critical realism and Kant's transcendental idealism

> But he who undertakes to judge, or still more, to construct, a system of Metaphysics, must satisfy the demands here made, either by adopting my solution, or by thoroughly refuting it, and substituting another. To evade it is impossible.
>
> (Immanuel Kant, *Prolegomena to any Future Metaphysics*)[66]

What is interesting about contemporary anti-realism is that for the most part its proponents do not take themselves to be idealists. Thus the defining claim tends not to be that consciousness or an objective conceptual order is ontologically basic, but rather that the only reality that we can coherently *talk* about is one that has already been structured by our subjective capacities and objective activities. This raises the question of just what it is that is being denied by those who understand themselves to be rejecting metaphysical realism but not to be endorsing idealism – and, conversely, what it is that is being affirmed by thinkers such as Bhaskar, Harré and Madden and Brian Ellis.

The question points us to Kant. The original, paradigmatic formulation of the idea that we don't just wish the world into existence, yet at the same time can only know it as it is for us, is Kant's. If transcendental realism is to be considered a viable alternative to post-positivist perspectivism, then Bhaskar will have to be able respond to Kant's transcendental idealism. If it turns out that he can, then there will be an opening for a critique of contemporary variants of Kant's approach. Bhaskar proceeds as though a lengthy discussion of Kant is unnecessary – Kant adhering, in Bhaskar's view, to an essentially

---

66 Immanuel Kant (trans. Paul Carus) *Prolegomena to Any Future Metaphysics that Can Qualify as a Science*, La Salle, IL: Open Court Publishing Company, 1902, 6th printing, 1988, p. 12.

Humean ontology. As I argue here, I think that Kant deserves individual attention. My purpose in the present chapter, therefore, is to try to assess whether or not critical realism does indeed provide a compelling line of response to transcendental idealism.

In the *Critique of Pure Reason* (1997) Kant presents us with a fundamental distinction. There are two ways that we can think about objects, he says.[67] On the one hand, we can engage in a kind of speculative flight of fancy, in which we try to imagine an object as it exists on its own, unrelated to us.[68] On the other hand, we can attempt to attain empirical knowledge of the object. If the latter, we must think of the object not as it is on its own, but as it is as a possible object of knowledge for us. Now, in the empiricist tradition, the distinction between objects considered in and of themselves and objects considered in light of how we may experience them is handled in just the opposite way. For an empiricist, those features that objects have that are relevant only "for us" can and must be disregarded. Indeed, it is the mark of sound thinking to do so. For empiricists, such "secondary qualities" are essentially misinterpretations of sensory experience. I perceive the flowers on my table as light yellow and fuschia, and incorrectly conclude from this that the flowers themselves are imbued with the properties of yellow-ness and red-ness. In reality, all that can be said of my flowers is that they reflect light in particular wavelengths.[69] From an empiricist perspective, then, Kant has got it backwards: it is precisely those properties that things only appear to have, given our particular perceptual apparatus, but which we falsely ascribe to them, that are in some sense "imaginary." If we want to *know* about a thing, we must consider it as it is apart from us.

But not so for Kant. For Kant, things considered as potential objects of knowledge necessarily bear the mark of our subjectivity. There are two reasons for this. The first has to do with the synthetic nature of perception. Kant holds that in order for an object to be something that can be known – as opposed to being something that can merely be an object of speculation – it must be such that, in

---

67 My understanding of Kant's position in *The Critique of Pure Reason* is greatly influenced by Arthur Collins's *Possible Experience: Understanding Kant's Critique of Pure Reason*, Berkeley: University of California Press, 1999. Following Collins, I take Kant to be a realist – an ambiguous and atypical sort of realist, but a realist all the same.

68 I am using words such as "object," "think" and "imagine" in their ordinary sense here, rather than in their specialized Kantian sense.

69 In this case, Kant would agree; the example of secondary qualities is only an analogy for the notion of the pure forms of intuition.

principle, it can be perceived.[70] This is a belief Kant shares with proponents of empiricism. But perception, according to Kant, is not the passive registration of input that empiricists say it is. Instead, perception consists in the application of what he calls the "pure forms of intuition," namely, space and time, to that which impinges upon our senses. To be clear, Kant does not mean by this that external stimuli cause an empiricist-like proto-perception, which is then further refined. Rather, the claim is that to perceive is to immediately and necessarily perceive objects as located in space and time. There can be no such thing as sensory input that is not mediated in this way, says Kant. However, the fact that we necessarily perceive objects in spatial and temporal terms is entirely a fact about *us*, about the structure of our experience qua bearers of reason; it has nothing to do with the nature of the external world itself, considered apart from us. (Or if it does, we can't know about it one way or another – for to consider objects as they are on their own would precisely be to think of them as existing outside of the context of space and time.)

The second reason why potential objects of knowledge must be thought of as objects-for-us has to do with the synthetic nature not just of perception, but of cognition. Cognition – or, knowledge – Kant says, involves the integration of the (synthetic) products of sense perception with what Kant calls the "Categories of the Understanding." As with perception, the claim is that the very process of cognition necessarily structures our experience. The key Category, for the purposes of the present discussion, is that of causality. Just as we cannot help but *perceive* objects as located in space and time, Kant says, we cannot help but *conceive* of events as having causal antecedents. And (crucially), as is the case with space and time, what we call "causality" must be understood to be a feature of reason itself, rather than to be a feature of the external world. Specifically, causality is the synthetic, a priori rule: "Every event has a cause."

Kant was interested in the question "What makes scientific knowledge possible?" There are differences of opinion regarding the meaning of this question. On the one hand, Kant is commonly taken to have been addressing the problem of skepticism – that is, of how, after Hume, scientific knowledge can be considered to be true. On the other hand, George Brittan, for example, argues that Kant's concern

---

70 Immanuel Kant (trans. and ed. Paul Guyer and Allen W. Wood), *Critique of Pure Reason*, New York: Cambridge University Press, 1997. Kant states this clearly at Pt. II, Div. I, Bk. II, Ch. II, Section III, <A225>, <B272–3>, among other places.

was rather to provide for a realist interpretation of the Newtonian physics of his day.[71] From this perspective, the emphasis is ontological rather than epistemic: Kant's question becomes "How is it possible that physics applies, as it patently does, to non-mental entities?" In terms that are hopefully general enough to side-step such debates, we may say at a minimum that what makes it possible operationally, according to Kant, for us to have the empirical knowledge that we do seem to have is the synthetic processes that I have just described: the constitution, via the Pure Forms of Intuition, of objects-as-we-cannot-help-but-perceive-them, and the structuring of our experience of such objects via the Categories of the Understanding. Kant called this position "transcendental idealism," and paired it with a commitment to what he termed "empirical realism."

Kant clearly distinguishes transcendental idealism from what he calls the "empirical idealism of Descartes" or the "mystical and visionary idealism of Berkeley."[72] "Material idealism," as Kant calls the generic position in the Refutation of Idealism, is "the theory that declares the existence of objects in space outside us to be either merely doubtful and indemonstrable, or else false and impossible."[73] Kant explicitly and adamantly rejects such a position. In the Refutation of Idealism, he argues that the very self-consciousness that Descartes treated as foundational presupposes the existence of the external, non-mental entities that Descartes would initially have us doubt.[74] (Berkeley's position, meanwhile, Kant takes himself to have rejected via his, Kant's, discussion of space in the Transcendental Aesthetic.)[75] He also rejects idealism through his account of the Pure Forms of Intuition. Although he takes space and time to be features of human subjectivity itself, Kant believes that they are brought to bear upon something external, something that pre-exists our perceptions of it. While the nature of this "something" can only be known empirically, and therefore only in terms that conform with the structure of reason, the fact of its existence is something that Kant takes as a given. This point is made quite forcefully in the *Prolegomena*, where Kant responds repeatedly to those who have misread him, he says, as being a proponent of idealism. It is worth quoting Kant at length:

71 See George Brittan Jr, *Kant's Theory of Science*, Princeton: Princeton University Press, 1978.

72 Kant, *Prolegomena*, First Part of the Transcendental Problem, Remark III, pp. 48–49.

73 Kant, *Critique of Pure Reason*, Pt. II, Div. I, Bk. II, Ch. II, Section III <B274>, p. 326.

74 Ibid., Section III <B275>, pp. 326–327.

75 Ibid., Section III <B274>.

Idealism consists in the assertion, that there are none but thinking beings, all other things, which we think are perceived in intuition, being nothing but representations in the thinking beings, to which no object external to them corresponds in fact. Whereas I say, that things as objects of our senses existing outside us are given, but we know nothing of what they may be in themselves, knowing only their appearances, i.e., the representations which they cause in us by affecting our senses. Consequently I grant by all means that there are bodies without us, that is, things which, though quite unknown to us as to what they are in themselves, we yet know by the representations which their influence on our sensibility procures us, and which we call bodies, a term signifying merely the appearance of the thing which is unknown to us, but not therefore less actual. Can this be termed idealism? It is the very contrary.[76]

Kant even proposes there that transcendental idealism be renamed critical idealism, if to do so will help to clarify his position on the issue.[77]

There is no question, then, that Kant believed in a physical reality. What is confusing, I think, is his insistence on the limited parameters of knowledge, and the vocabulary that he uses to express such limitation. As noted above, Kant tells us that that although there is surely something which impinges upon our senses from without, to perceive an object is nonetheless already to have acted upon it, cognitively, such that the mind is able to recognize it *as* an object. It is thus in the very nature of the case that we cannot get beyond such "representations," as Kant calls the products of perception. Unfortunately, Kant's language is potentially misleading, because it makes it sound as though he is advancing the view that the only things that we can know are our own sensory or mental impressions. But Kant makes it plain that he does not believe that we are trapped inside our own minds, cut off from all but our own internal thoughts and perceptions.[78] The contention is simply that the objects of empirical knowledge have already been given shape and temporal

---

76 Kant, *Prolegomena*, First Part of the Transcendental Problem, Remark II, p. 43.
77 Ibid., Remark III, p. 49.
78 This way of putting it I attribute to Arthur Collins. The underlying thesis of Collins's book is that Kant is misread because he is assumed to be working within a Cartesian framework, in the context of which the task is to get from inner experience, of which we can be certain, to outer experience, which has been cast in doubt. Op. cit., Collins, *Possible Experience*.

location through the very process of perception.[79] There is no way around this, in Kant's view, because Kant does not consider thought that has no possible empirical content (i.e., thought that is not perceptually based) to *be* knowledge. Thus he writes: "thinking of an object in general through a pure concept of the understanding can become cognition only insofar as this concept is related to objects of the senses."[80] Knowledge must be empirically grounded. Such grounding, however, is necessarily mediated by the Pure Forms of Intuition. Ironically, then, it is only because Kant is so exacting in his opposition to rationalism that he is mistaken for a subjective idealist.

If one takes Kant's stated opposition to idealism seriously, then what is questionable in his account of the conditions of possibility of natural science cannot be any lack of commitment on Kant's part to the existence of an external, non-mental reality. What, then, is the difference between transcendental idealism and transcendental realism? I want to pursue this question further, and in a different manner, than Bhaskar himself does. The following is thus a rational reconstruction – and in places a modification – of Bhaskar's views, rather than a summary.

A transcendental realist response to Kant can be constructed around three main points. To begin, Bhaskar claims that Kant's theory of causality is unsatisfactory. Kant's reply to Hume was that the necessity of the causal relationship is not a matter of subjective expectation, or habit, but rather an intrinsic feature of reason itself. Bhaskar's response is that Kant fails as surely as Hume does to account for the practice of experimentation. The argument against Hume must be refined, however, in order to apply to Kant. As in the critique of Hume, we begin with the widely accepted assumption that experiments allow us to determine what the cause of x is by providing a controlled environment in which it is possible to isolate and potentially activate different causal variables. The problem with Kant's definition of causality is that if causality were what he says it is – namely, an a priori relationship ascribed to all relata necessarily – then it is not clear why our knowledge of such relationships would be enhanced by the creation of artificial environments. Rendering open systems closed should not help us to narrow in on necessary causal connections if the necessity of such connections is an a priori feature of reason.

A defender of Kant might be expected to respond, first, that in part the function of creating controlled experimental settings is to

---

79 See Collins, *Possible Experience*, Ch. 5, for an effective presentation of this point.
80 Kant, *Critique of Pure Reason*, Pt. II, Div. I, Bk. I, Ch. II., Section II <B146>, p. 254.

keep people's beliefs, prejudices, and non-cognitive objectives from interfering with scientific inquiry. Such measures are entirely consistent with transcendental idealism. After all, causality is not a matter of the particular beliefs of any one, or even all, individuals. It is rather a feature of all thought whatsoever, about the world as we experience it. Beyond this general point, the defender of Kant would say that the a priori condition that we cannot but experience events as having causes tells us nothing about which actual events have which actual causes. Which x causes which y, he or she would say, is a purely empirical matter, open to scientific investigation to determine.

For the transcendental realist, however, it is not clear what the *significance* would be of such a determination, construed in Kantian terms. If causality itself is nothing but a feature of reason, a way that we cannot help but experience the world, then the very concept of a "cause" loses its force (literally). To put it differently, if the causal nature of causal connections is provided by the faculty of reason, rather than by real properties of the antecedent, then to say of the antecedent that it is the "cause" of that which follows is simply to say that it is the first in a specified sequence of events – that whenever it is present, the event with which it is associated will also be present. Kant is no more entitled to speak of "causes" in an everyday way, to mean "that which brought about a given outcome" than was Hume. Both are obliged to do away with "causes" understood as entities endowed with dispositional properties. As it was for Hume, to be the "cause" of x is, for Kant, merely to be constantly conjoined with x.

The Kantian will object. To be the "cause" of something, he or she will say, is to be that which *must* come first – and this, he or she will add, is a matter that must be established empirically. But the Kantian can't have it both ways. The necessity in question (the "must," upon which the Kantian interlocutor insists) is, for Kant, a *transcendental* necessity; it is what allows us to formulate *all* causal claims. As a *transcendental* necessity, it tells us nothing about what it means to say, at the empirical level, that x, and not z, is "the cause" of y. It is of no help at the empirical level because it "applies," in some sense, to *all* posited regularities – those that are in fact coincidental and those that truly are the result of a causal connection – with equal force.[81] I

81 The claim here is at a different level of abstraction from the claim that Kant's transcendental necessity doesn't tell us which x causes which y. Here the claim is that a transcendental necessity of the sort that Kant proposes doesn't tell us any more than Hume's constant conjunctions did about what it is to *be* the x that causes y.

don't see any way around it. The Kantian must accept the implications at the level of empirical inquiry of (a) rejecting the concept of natural necessity, and (b) adopting a specifically transcendental alternative. To forswear the concept of natural necessity is to maintain that there is nothing about the antecedent itself that gives rise to the necessity of its conjunction with a given consequent. And again, if there is nothing about the antecedent itself that renders it the "cause" of the consequent, then at the level of empirical inquiry we are exactly where Hume left us. While causality is no longer merely a matter of subjective expectation, a cause is still nothing other than "that which comes first in an identified sequence."

Let us return to the phenomenon of experimentation. When the Kantian tells us that it is through empirical investigation that we find out which x causes which y, he or she is implicitly asserting one or both of the following: (a) that experiments are a way of helping us to determine which Judgments of Experience are valid, and/or (b) that experiments are a way of helping us get from Judgments of Perception to valid Judgments of Experience, to use the language of the *Prolegomena*. But the Kantian cannot say why or how this should be so. The Kantian differs from the Humean in that, unlike the Humean, the Kantian is prepared to distinguish between regularities (i.e., Judgments of Perception) and regularities that are necessary (i.e., Judgments of Experience). The problem, however, is that a purely transcendental conception of causality simply does not authorize such a distinction. The Kantian can tell us that we cannot help but *make* the distinction (for this is simply another way of saying that we cannot help but conceive of the world as causally ordered, i.e., that we cannot conceive of it except via the Category of Causality), but, having dispensed with the idea of natural necessity, he or she cannot give meaning to it. Kant may very well be right that we necessarily conceptualize the world in causal terms, but this alone cannot sustain an account of science.

Bhaskar's second major objection to transcendental idealism is related to the first. Specifically, Bhaskar criticizes transcendental idealists for following Hume in treating the constant conjunction of events as a necessary – if in Kant's case necessary but not sufficient – component of a scientific law. Hume saw scientific laws as the registration of perceived regularities. His stunning claim was that our belief in the necessity of such regularities is philosophically unfounded, that the very concept of natural necessity is in reality a projection of our own subjective expectation that what has happened in the past will happen in the same way in the future. Kant could not abide such a radically unstable and subjectivist view of natural science. Instead, he proposed that observed connections between the objects that we perceive are a priori necessary in the sense described earlier. But while Kant re-introduces necessity into the empiricist picture, he nonetheless retains the idea that what scientific laws apply to is perceived constant conjunctions. Kant's similarity to Hume in this respect is especially clear in the *Prolegomena*, where one can see the way in which Kant has taken on the task of establishing the necessity of causal connections between "representations." Thus Kant writes:

> As an easier example, we may take the following: "When the sun shines on the stone, it grows warm." This judgment, however often I and others may have perceived it, is a mere judgment of perception, and contains no necessity; perceptions are only usually conjoined in this manner. But if I say, "The sun warms the stone," I add to the perception a concept of the understanding, viz., that of cause, which connects with the concept of sunshine that of heat as a necessary consequence, and the synthetical jugment becomes of necessity universally valid, viz., objective, and is converted from a perception into experience.[82]

As described in Chapter 1, one of the central claims of *RTS* is that it is mistake to think that a constant conjunction of events is a requisite condition of a scientific law. The argument, again, is that scientists engage in experimentation precisely because regularities do not generally occur in open, or naturally unfolding, settings. The very fact that regularities have to be artificially produced, however, implies (assuming that experimentation is what it is commonly thought to be) that they must be distinguishable from laws. If experimentation is what we think it is, then it cannot be that in producing constant conjunctions between given events, scientists simultaneously produce the laws that govern them. Instead, it must be that laws are statements not of regularities (which can be artificially produced), but rather of the underlying mechanisms that account for them. Bhaskar's argument is that it follows from this that regularities are neither sufficient, as the Humean would have it, nor even necessary, as the Kantian would maintain, for the formulation of a scientific law.

Finally, Bhaskar accuses Kant of having committed the epistemic fallacy. As noted earlier, the epistemic fallacy is the wrongful reduction, or translation, of ontological questions into epistemological questions. While the posing of any question is undeniably an epistemological act – and as such an element of the transitive rather

---

82 Kant, *Prolegomena*, p. 59, note 1.

than the intransitive dimension of science – it is nonetheless both possible and crucially important, according to Bhaskar, to distinguish between questions about being and questions about our knowledge (or lack thereof) of being. To conflate the two – apart from being a category mistake – is to engage in the worst sort of subjectivist anthropomorphism. Our existence, and by extension our knowledge of the circumstances in which we find ourselves, is entirely contingent, Bhaskar insists; there could quite easily have been a natural world that did not include human beings – just as, to the best of our knowledge, was the case for most of the earth's history.[83]

Before anything can be decided about Kant and the epistemic fallacy, however, a preliminary discussion of Bhaskar's approach is in order. Bhaskar's argument in *RTS* is that Kant has committed the epistemic fallacy by virtue of being what Bhaskar terms an empirical realist. It is worth noting that while Kant too characterizes himself as defending a position that he too calls empirical realism, he and Bhaskar do not ascribe the same meaning to the term. For Kant, an empirical realist is someone who believes that the objects of our experience are real, that they are not merely the products of our thoughts. Empirical realism as Kant uses the term is thus a form of materialism, to be contrasted with subjective idealism. As Bhaskar defines it, by contrast, empirical realism is ultimately the view that the only objects that exist are those that have been perceived. Empirical realism so construed is thus a prime example of subjective idealism. Bhaskar seems to believe that Kant is an empirical realist of this sort.

Bhaskar can be seen as identifying two relevant problems with empirical realism as he conceives it. For the sake of convenience, I will dub the first one ontological and the second one epistemological. The ontological problem is that empirical realists, by definition, from Bhaskar's perspective, presume that the category of reality is exhausted by the category of experience. The idea that reality is coterminous with experience leads empirical realists to hold a severely truncated, and therefore fatally flawed, ontology. As a transcendental rather than an empirical realist, Bhaskar, by contrast, maintains that experience is only the top level of a "stratified" reality that is characterized, above all, by what he refers to as "depth." The epistemological problem, meanwhile, is that empirical realism involves the view that what scientific laws describe are constant conjunctions. Bhaskar's contention is that laws do not refer to such

---

83 Bhaskar, *RTS*, p. 22, p. 29 and *passim*. Bhaskar makes this point repeatedly, in a variety of different ways.

sequences at all, but rather to underlying causal mechanisms – that is, to the powers of real entities to effect change.

If the epistemic fallacy is the turning of statements about being into statements about our knowledge of being, then proponents of empirical realism as Bhaskar defines it commit the fallacy both indirectly, via their ontology, and directly, via their account of scientific laws. In the ontological case, the epistemic fallacy is committed because reality itself is reduced to the totality of that which has been experienced – that is, to the domain of the Empirical. In the epistemological case, the epistemic fallacy is committed directly, in as much as scientific laws are understood to be descriptions of perceived regularities rather than accounts of the causal powers of objects. Statements about being (or what *should* be statements about being) are thus reduced to statements about our perceptions of being.

Bhaskar would have it that Kant, like Hume, commits the epistemic fallacy in virtue of his adherence to empirical realism as Bhaskar conceives it. Kant, Bhaskar says,

> committed it in arguing that the categories "allow only of empirical employment and have no meaning whatsoever when not applied to objects of possible experience; that is to the world of sense." (For us on the other hand if the Kantian categories were adequate to the objects of scientific thought then they would continue to apply in a world without sense, and have a meaning in relation to that possibility.)[84]

I am not convinced that this is the best way to present the case against Kant. With respect to the question of whether or not Kant regards reality as coterminous with experience, there are several points to be made. First, Kant is plainly committed to the existence of non-mental entities. If he is guilty of having committed the epistemic fallacy on ontological grounds, it cannot be because he thinks that reality is "nothing other" than a set of individually or collectively borne perceptual states. Second, if the "experience" in question is understood empirically, to mean "the actual experience, by a subject, of a given object," then, again, the charge does not apply to Kant. When Kant says that knowledge must be tied to experience, he does not mean that we can only know that with which we have had personal sensory contact. Rather, he means that we can only have knowledge of that which we could *in principle* experience. Finally, even if the assertion is that Kant commits the epistemic fallacy in

---

84 Bhaskar, *RTS*, p. 37.

virtue of his empirical realism because he identifies reality with that which *in principle* can be experienced, it is incorrect. Kant doesn't say that the only objects that *exist* are those that can (in principle) be perceived; he says that the only objects that we can have *knowledge* of (as opposed to speculate about) are those that can (in principle) be perceived.

The epistemological charge, again, was that empirical realists reduce questions about being to questions about our knowledge of being because they understand scientific laws to be descriptions of sequences of perceptual events, rather than statements about the powers of entities. But this is not how a Kantian conceptualizes scientific laws. Although, like the empiricist, a transcendental idealist sees scientific laws as *applying* to sequences of events, the transcendental idealist does not *identify* the law with the sequence. Kant is a non-realist with respect to causality, true, but on the matter of whether or not scientific laws *reduce* to contingent subjective experience, or statements thereof, his response is "No."

Admittedly, what Bhaskar focuses on is Kant's claim that empirical knowledge must be based in experience. Kant may be understood as saying only those things that can be directly perceived may be objects of knowledge. Bhaskar's view, by contrast, is that we can and do make legitimate knowledge claims about objects that we *cannot* directly perceive. (Indeed, his contention is that attempting to identify underlying-but-not-necessarily-empirically-manifest processes – rather than merely describing observable events – is precisely what scientists do.) Given ample indirect evidence for the existence of electrons, for example, it was perfectly acceptable, from Bhaskar's perspective, not to have waited until the invention of powerful microscopes to incorporate them into scientific theory.[85] If, as Kant would have it, we declare that it is by definition impossible to have knowledge of objects that we cannot directly perceive, then we are forced to conclude either (a) that scientific knowledge may not out-step current levels of observational technology, or (b) that scientific knowledge is not empirically based, and is therefore not knowledge at all.

This is a significant line of criticism directed at Kant on the basis of his empirical realism. Kant does reduce "empirical" to "empiricist" in his conception of the object-domain of knowledge, and his affinity with empiricists on this issue is a major, and important, point of difference between transcendental idealism and transcendental realism. Still, it does not follow from Kant's strictures regarding what kinds of objects can be known, as opposed to only be thought about, that

---

85 Note that highly technologically mediated "observation" is largely inferential.

Kant has committed the epistemic fallacy – for in telling us that it is only possible to have knowledge of those objects that we can experience, Kant has not said that it is only possible to have knowledge of knowledge (or of subjective experience). If Kant has committed the epistemic fallacy, then it is on different grounds than has Hume. Specifically, if Kant has committed the epistemic fallacy, then it is by virtue (or at least primarily by virtue) of his transcendental idealism rather than his empirical realism (as either he or Bhaskar defines it).

And has he done so? The answer is both "Yes" and "No," it seems to me, depending on how the epistemic fallacy is construed. While I have so far proceeded as though Bhaskar offers a single definition of the concept, and employs it consistently, I don't think that such is actually the case. Instead, there are at least four different accounts of the epistemic fallacy at play in *RTS*, only some of which apply to Kant – even when properly evaluated in light of his transcendental idealism rather than his empirical realism.

The epistemic fallacy is first depicted as having been committed when questions about being are transposed into questions about our knowledge of being. Thus the question "Does x exist?" becomes, via the epistemic fallacy, the question "What is the nature of our knowledge of x?"[86] In this initial formulation, the mistake that is alleged to have been made is what I will call an epistemological one: an entire class of questions has been incorrectly disallowed. The epistemic fallacy is thus a kind of methodological error at the level of meta-theory.

The second account of the concept comes through Bhaskar's discussion of the three "domains" of the stratified critical realist ontology. Here the epistemic fallacy is committed when the domain of the Real is identified with the domain of the Empirical. In this case, the problem is not that the thinker who has committed the fallacy has transposed a question about what exists into a question about our knowledge of what exists, but rather that he or she has inadvertently lopped off a large portion of reality by saying that the only things that exist are either (a) the things that we perceive through our senses or (b) our sensations themselves. In this second formulation, the mistake that has been made is what I therefore will call an ontological one: the epistemic fallacy amounts to the adoption of a grossly deficient ontology.

Third, Bhaskar approaches the concept of the epistemic fallacy through the issue of scientific laws. Empiricists believe that natural scientific laws refer in the end to regularities in our perceptual fields.

---

86 The post-structuralist version of the transposition, namely, "How is x discursively constructed?" Bhaskar terms the linguistic fallacy.

Bhaskar's view is that scientific laws refer not to perceptual regularities (or even to regular sequences of "external" events), but rather to causal powers – to the dispositional properties that things have the capacity to display.[87] In this case, the epistemic fallacy is committed when scientific laws are mistakenly thought to refer to "subjective" features of our experience rather than to "objective" properties of entities. Here I would again characterize the fallacy as an epistemological one, though it is so in a different sense than in the foregoing version. In this case, the thinker who has committed the epistemic fallacy has misconceived a particular sort of explanatory concept (namely, a "law").

Finally, Bhaskar also presents the idea of the epistemic fallacy through the analysis of causality. Here the epistemic fallacy is committed when causality is mistakenly believed to be either an expectation, as in Hume, or, as in Kant, an a priori category of reason itself. The error in this case is ontological: the thinker who commits the epistemic fallacy does not appreciate that causality is a feature of the physical world, operative in virtue of the real powers of entities.

My view is that Kant commits versions one, three and four of the epistemic fallacy, but not version two. Moreover, the claim that he commits versions three and four must be qualified. That he commits version one is obvious. Version one is little else than Kant's "Copernican turn," cast as a formal error of reason. Not only does it apply to Kant, it represents Kant's distinctive and innovative contribution to the history of Western philosophy; the only real question is whether or not it is a fallacy. But even here, where the case for Kant having committed what Bhaskar rightly or wrongly terms the epistemic fallacy seems self-evident, it is important to proceed with care. Kant's meta-philosophical injunction that we reject speculative metaphysics and engage instead in the critique of reason is a directive about how to do *philosophy*, not about how to do science. Kant transposes metaphysical questions about "Being" into questions about the conditions of, and limits to, knowledge, but he does not thereby transpose scientific questions about the behavior of objects into questions about the conditions of and limits to our knowledge of such objects. It is true that at the ontic level (or what

---

87 In the Appendix to *RTS* Bhaskar notes that in the text he used the term "law" to refer both to causal mechanisms and to statements that refer to them. He comments that if he were to do it over again, he would reserve the term "law" for the mechanisms in nature, and would not use it to refer to statements about such mechanisms. I use the term to refer to certain kinds of statements. I believe that to do so is actually most in keeping with the overall thrust of Bhaskar's thinking.

Kant, though not Bhaskar, would call the empirical level), the level of
scientific inquiry, Kant will say that objects of knowledge (as opposed
to objects of pure thought) are always and only objects as we cannot
help but perceive them (i.e., situated in space and time) and conceive
them (e.g., as causally related), but this is hardly to say that our
questions about such objects are or ought to be self-reflexive questions about our own capacities for reason. The latter are the purview
of philosophy, for Kant, not science.

One might respond that I have been too stringent in my interpretation of this verson of the epistemic fallacy. What if, in particular at
the empirical level, we understand "The transposition of questions
about Being into questions about our knowledge of Being" to mean,
not "into questions about our own perceptual and cognitive processes," but merely "into questions about the state of our knowledge
of objects?" Formulated in this way, is Kant not a proponent of the
epistemic fallacy at the empirical as well as the transcendental level? I
still don't think so. We are talking now about a proposition to the
effect that claims about objects in the world ought to be understood
to be claims about our *knowledge* of objects in the world. Such a
position can be understood in one of two ways, it seems to me. On
the one hand, the point may be that there is an unbridgeable divide
between our theories and that to which they refer, such that
ultimately we can only ever have knowledge of the former. On the
other hand, the point may simply be the unexceptional one that there
is no way to have knowledge of a thing except by having knowledge
of it.

If Kant commits version one of the epistemic fallacy at the level of
scientific inquiry, then he does so in the second sense only. Kant is
neither an idealist nor a skeptic. There is no question for him but that
our theories about the world tell us something about what the world
is like.[88] Of course, here one might respond that if Kant believes that
theories tell us about the objects to which they refer, then it is only
because he has already "subjectivized" the objects. But I don't think
that this is entirely the right way to put it. Again, Kant's view is not
that we cannot know the external world, but rather that the only way
to think scientifically about objects is to regard them as they must be
in order to be objects of knowledge for us in the first place (and not
simply objects of speculation). As already suggested, Kant distinguishes between what he calls "representations" and what he calls
"things in themselves," not for the purpose of advancing a non-realist

---

88 Brittan, op. cit., argues that Kant's main purpose in his works on epistemology
and metaphysics was to provide a realist interpretation of Newtonian physics.

account of scientific inquiry, but rather for the purpose of differentiating between science and metaphysics. Meanwhile, the fact that our best answers to empirical questions[89] are themselves knowledge claims is of no great consequence for Kant – as it is not for Bhaskar.

Version two of the epistemic fallacy has it that the epistemic fallacy is a matter of identifying that which exists with that which is experienced. I have already argued that this is not true of Kant. Kant does claim that we can only have *knowledge* of that which we can (in principle) perceive directly. This is a huge concession to classical empiricism, and one to which Bhaskar is opposed. Even so, it is hardly to say that only that to which we have gained a very specific sort of cognitive access actually *exists*. Kant may have set limits regarding the sorts of objects in relation to which intelligible knowledge claims may be advanced, but the limits are entirely epistemic. That we can only have knowledge of a particular class of objects does not imply that the only objects that exist are those that we can know. A Kantian might argue that I am coming dangerously close here to missing the whole point of Kant's intervention. But Kant does save room for the existence of things that exist but in principle cannot be accessed empirically. We can think about such things; we can have faith in such things; we just can't have empirical knowledge of such things.

Version three is that the epistemic fallacy consists of reducing scientific laws to statements regarding the constant conjunction of perceived events. I argued earlier that if Kant is guilty of this, then it is not by virtue of a commitment to what either he or Bhaskar call empirical realism. The question, then, is whether or not this version of the epistemic fallacy follows from Kant's transcendental idealism. I would say that the answer is yes, but with certain important qualifications. From Kant's perspective, a scientific law is a rule-like statement about regularities in the world. While it is true that it is the constant conjunction of perceivable events to which laws *apply*, this is not to say that laws are simply statements of such conjunctions. Kant makes this point very clearly in the *Prolegomena* when he distinguishes between what he calls "Judgments of Perception" and "Judgments of Experience."[90] The claim there is that it is only Judgments of Experience that involve the idea of a necessary connection between antecedent and consequent. To be fair, Bhaskar does acknowledge that for Kant regularity is merely a necessary component of the concept of a law – as opposed to being both necessary and sufficient, as it is for Hume. And admittedly, the

89 That is, what Bhaskar might call substantive scientific questions.
90 Kant, *Prolegomena*, pp. 55–58.

specification of "Judgments of Experience" is part of the very discussion that, in another light, shows just how much of the Humean problematic Kant has taken on. Clearly the advantage of grouping Kant and Hume together is that the distinctiveness of Bhaskar's own conception of scientific law is all the more evident. But while it is important to emphasize that Bhaskar breaks with both Kant and Hume in divorcing the concept of a law from the concept of regularity, it is also important to keep in mind the differences between transcendental idealism and empiricism. And while it is true, as I have maintained, that in Kant's view causality itself is a rubric that is generated by us (and is not intrinsic to the external world, considered apart from us), I would reiterate that for Kant this does not imply that scientific laws are statements about the contingent subjective experience of individual knowers. Ultimately, though, Kant commits version three of the epistemic fallacy in the following sense: he believes that the necessary relationships that are identified by scientific laws derive the necessity that they do have from reason itself rather than from the powers that inhere in things.

In the end, Kant also commits what I have called version four of the epistemic fallacy. In version four, the epistemic fallacy is a matter of misconceiving the phenomenon of causality. Kant believes causality to be a feature of reason rather than to be the exercise or display of powers that entities have to effect change. Although the transcendental idealist form of this version of the fallacy is different from the empiricist form, the Kantian variant does constitute a non-naturalist, conception of causality. From the perspective of transcendental realism, an error has been made. Kant has improperly rendered causality a function of the exercise of reason.

Let me step back for a moment. I began this discussion by proposing that, from the perspective of a rational reconstruction of *RTS*, there are at least three major points of disagreement between Bhaskar and Kant: Bhaskar believes Kant to be mistaken about the nature of causality; Bhaskar believes Kant to therefore hold to an inadequate conception of scientific law; Bhaskar believes Kant to have committed what he, Bhaskar, calls the epistemic fallacy. The objections are inter-related. The first two may be thought of as referring to the objective and subjective expressions, respectively, of the same philosophical problem. The third, meanwhile, in part is simply a restatement of the first two, under the heading "epistemic fallacy." It is also, however, a rejection of the particular line that Kant draws between knowledge and speculative metaphysics. The question to ask now is whether or not the critique of transcendental idealism is sound. Before doing so, however, let me offer two final observations.

The first is that Bhaskar and Kant agree about a number of very basic things, and it is important not to lose sight of this. Neither Bhaskar nor Kant is a subjective idealist. (Neither the early Bhaskar nor Kant is an objective idealist either, for that matter.) In different ways, both Bhaskar and Kant find that the adoption of an empiricist theory of knowledge is related to an acceptance of the subjective idealist ontology which both take to be incorrect. Neither is a rationalist. In different ways, both take science to be an empirical though not empiricist endeavor; both believe it to be a rational attempt to understand the way the world operates; both believe that the accepted natural science of their day constitutes a valid body of knowledge. Finally, both Bhaskar and Kant engage in versions of transcendental argumentation. Kant begins with what he takes to be absolutely true scientific knowledge about the world, and asks what must be the case in order for it to be possible for us to have such knowledge. Bhaskar begins with the acknowledged necessity of experimentation for the pursuit of what he takes to be fallibilistically, or provisionally, true scientific knowledge about the world, and asks what must be the case in order for experiments to be and do what they are regularly taken to be and do.

Meanwhile, there are – as we have seen – significant differences between the two. I have presented these in some detail. So far, however, I have approached the contrast from the point of view of transcendental realism. The second point that I want to make here is that from the perspective of transcendental idealism, transcendental realism is inadequate in ways that are not even on the table. Indeed, Kant would say that Bhaskar has failed to address the most basic of philosophical questions associated with the idea that we are successful in coming to know the world. Bhaskar has no real theory of cognition, of how it is that we are able in the first place to ask anything at all of our surroundings. Nor does Bhaskar offer much of an account of perception. Moreover, from a Kantian perspective, Bhaskar, unlike Kant, has made no philosophical effort to establish the rationality of scientific practice or the conceptual products thereof. In this regard, there is a real sense in which *RTS* is simply an elaboration of the ontological presuppositions of Baconian experimentation, rather than a reflection on the question of why we should take scientific theory seriously, or assume that our findings apply to the physical world. To put it differently, while Bhaskar and Kant both begin with a presumption about the rationality of science, Kant then reasons backwards, as it were, in an effort to defend the presumption philosophically. Bhaskar, by contrast, makes no such effort. Instead, he goes on to ask what the general features of the world must be, given that we do regard experimentation to be a sound and necessary way of learning about it. From the perspective of transcendental idealism, transcendental realism therefore appears to be predicated on a naive, non-philosophical assertion of the legitimacy of science and its applicability to the world. It is, in the technical sense of the term, dogmatic.

Ultimately, however, the question is not whether or not Bhaskar has succeeded in doing what Kant set out to do, but rather whether or not Bhaskar has cast doubt on Kant's success in doing what *Kant* set out to do. The crux of Bhaskar's criticism is that Kant's account of necessity does not sustain the practice of natural science after all. On this fundamental point, I think that Bhaskar is persuasive. Although he does not focus his attention as closely or as protractedly on Kant as one might like, and although there are places where corrections are required, my view is that Bhaskar has made a strong case for adopting a transcendental realist, rather than transcendental idealist, stance towards causality and causal laws. There is also the matter of Kant's demarcation between science and metaphysics. Bhaskar, unlike Kant, seems to believe that it is possible to have knowledge of noumena (e.g., knowledge of freedom, of the soul or of God). However, this belief has little direct bearing on his understanding of science. For this reason, I don't believe that it is crucial to the discussion at hand. The more important contrast between Bhaskar and Kant concerns, not the distinction that Kant makes between noumena and phenomena, but the distinction that he makes between knowledge and "thought."[91] Unlike Kant, Bhaskar does not equate empirical knowledge with a body of statements, each of which is based on sense data. For Bhaskar, theoretical claims – as well as claims regarding unobservable entities and/or processes (often only presently unobservable) – that are developed in the context of natural scientific inquiry are an inextricable component of empirical knowledge. It may not be too much of a leap here to think of Quine's position on the matter – that science cannot be meaningfully resolved into a pile of empirical statements and a pile of analytic statements. This is an important difference between a transcendental realist conception of empirical knowledge and a Kantian conception. I believe that the transcendental realist account is a more promising theory of knowledge than is Kant's empiricist alternative. As the history of logical positivism strongly

---

91 I am following Arthur Collins in treating the distinction between the noumenal and the phenomenal realms as different from the distinction between objects considered as potential objects of knowledge and objects considered in and of themselves. Collins, *Possible Experience*, Ch. 4.

suggests, the divide between knowledge and thought is not as sharp as Kant would have it.

Finally, lest there be confusion regarding the idea that we can and do gain knowledge of things in themselves, I want to reiterate that Bhaskar maintains that our knowledge thereof is highly mediated. Kant's claim that we cannot investigate something without relating to it as a potential object of knowledge for us sets the bar to realism far lower by comparison. Just how Bhaskar handles the issue of mediation, however, is another question altogether. I will discuss it further when I turn to what I take to be the broadly Kantian challenge to realism to be found in the work of Hilary Putnam.

3 Natural kinds
Critical realism and Putnam's internal realism

In an effort to identify just what is in dispute in the debate over realism, I turned my attention in Chapter 2 to the differences between Bhaskar and Kant. I began with Kant because Bhaskar believes himself to have dispensed with Kant and because I believe Kant to have largely set the terms for subsequent opposition to what might be called unqualified metaphysical realism. I hope to have established that transcendental realism represents a serious response to Kant's challenge. The fundamental issue in question in relation to Kant is not realism about objects, but realism about causality. Bhaskar shows that a Kantian conception of causality is inadequate to the task that Kant set for himself. The idea that we cannot help but conceive of the world as causally ordered simply does not tell us what we need to know about the production of scientific knowledge.

In this chapter, I want to continue to explore the issues raised in Chapter 2 by introducing Hilary Putnam into the discussion. As in Chapter 2, my underlying objective is two-fold: first, to specify what it is that separates a transcendental realist such as Bhaskar from thinkers who would be critical of his stance yet do not take themselves to be idealists; second, to assess the viability of transcendental realism. I see the impetus of the previous chapter being carried forward in two ways. The first has to do with the theme of mediation. While Kant is not the first to suggest that cognition is a dynamic process in which the subject plays an active role – Aristotle comes to mind as an obvious predecessor – still, it is Kant who most forcefully introduces the idea that our knowledge necessarily bears the mark of our subjectivity. Putnam is centrally concerned with this key insight. The second way in which the present chapter is an extension of the last is that not only does Putnam operate within a generally Kantian philosophical universe, but he understands himself to be involved – at least the Putnam of the 1980s and early 1990s does – in a fairly straightforward appropriation of Kant's views.

Putnam is the author of the distinction between "metaphysical realism" and "internal realism." The now-classic formulation of the contrast between metaphysical and internal realism appears in Chapter 3 of *Reason, Truth and History*, entitled "Two Philosophical Perspectives."[92] Metaphysical realism, as Putnam would have it, is a philosophical stance comprising three basic principles: (1) ontological realism, (2) the idea that there is one and only one true and complete account of reality as a whole and (3) the correspondence theory of truth. To quote the familiar passage:

> One of these perspectives is the perspective of metaphysical realism. On this perspective, the world consists of some fixed totality of mind-independent objects. There is exactly one true and complete description of "the way the world is." Truth involves some sort of correspondence relation between words or thought-signs and external things and sets of things. I shall call this perspective the *externalist* perspective, because its favorite point of view is a God's Eye point of view.[93]

Putnam contrasts metaphysical realism, which he rejects, with internal realism, which he endorses. Internal realism is the combination of (1) an ontological quasi-realism, in which objects relative to any given conceptual scheme are taken to be real, (2) the idea that there are multiple true accounts of any given phenomenon and (3) a definition of truth as idealized rational acceptability. To quote Putnam again:

> . . . it is characteristic of this view to hold that *what objects does the world consist of?* is a question that it only makes sense to ask *within* a theory or description. Many "internalist" philosophers, though not all, hold further that there is more than one "true" theory or description of the world. "Truth," in an internalist view, is some sort of (idealized) rational acceptability – some sort of ideal coherence of our beliefs with each other and with our experiences *as those experiences are themselves represented in our belief system* – and not correspondence with mind-independent or discourse-independent "states of affairs."[94]

---

92 Hilary Putnam, *Reason, Truth and History*, Cambridge: Cambridge University Press, 1981.
93 Ibid., p. 49.
94 Ibid., pp. 49–50. Putnam's characterization of his own views on the concept of truth are somewhat ambiguous here. It is not entirely clear from this passage whether Putnam holds a consensus theory of truth or a coherence theory of truth. Linda Alcoff has claimed Putnam as a proponent of coherence (see Linda Martin Alcoff, *Real Knowing: New Versions of the Coherence Theory*, Ithaca, NY: Cornell University Press, 1996, Ch. 6.), and there is certainly something to this.

In *Scientific Realism and Human Emancipation*, Bhaskar refers to Putnam directly (albeit in a footnote), and says that he himself is going to defend a form of metaphysical realism.[95] I intend to discuss the differences between Bhaskar and Putnam's views at some length, but to begin I want to address the basic question of whether or not transcendental realism is in fact a form of metaphysical realism as Putnam has defined it. Bhaskar seems to think that the answer is yes. My view is that it is important to specify more precisely than this the extent to which Bhaskar's views do or do not fit the bill. The first component of metaphysical realism á la Putnam is ontological realism, construed as the belief that "the world consists of some fixed totality of mind-independent objects."[96] Given that Bhaskar does argue for the existence of mind-independent objects, it is fair to say that he is a Putnam-esque metaphysical realist in this regard. At the same time, however, Bhaskar would agree with the letter, if not the spirit, of Putnam's contention that *"what objects does the world consist of?* is a question that it only makes sense to ask *within* a theory or description."[97] It is also worth noting that the "objects" that Bhaskar takes to be ultimate are powers – indeed, potentialities –

On balance, however, Putnam talks about ideally warranted assent far more often than he does about coherence (e.g., "My own view is that truth is to be identified with idealized justification," in *Realism with a Human Face*, 1990, p. 115). For this reason I regard him as holding that it is the former, rather than the latter, which constitutes a *definition* of truth. Coherence is certainly a criterion of *justification*, however, for Putnam.

95 Bhaskar, *Scientific Realism and Human Emancipation*, p. 6 and footnote.

96 In a reply to critics Hartry Field and Gilbert Harman, published as "A Defense of Internal Realism," in Hilary Putnam, *Realism with a Human Face* (ed. James Conant), Cambridge, MA: Harvard University Press, 1990, pp. 30–42, Putnam insists that the three "tenets" of metaphysical realism, as I've been calling them, must be considered in conjunction with one another. "Metaphysical realisms *one*, *two* and *three* do not have content standing on their own, one by one; each leans on the others and on a variety of further assumptions and notions," he writes (p. 31). I appreciate that Putnam is undertaking to criticize what he takes to be not just a set of propositions, but an entire worldview, and one which is embedded in an intellectual historical context. Nonetheless, I think that he is wrong to say that ontological realism and the correspondence theory of truth, for example, have no content on their own and thus cannot be meaningfully disentangled from one another. And I can see no special connection between the correspondence theory, as opposed to any other non-relativist theory of truth (such as, e.g., the "idealized justification" theory propounded by Putnam), and the idea that there is only one true and complete account of the world. While I shall endeavor to be respectful of Putnam's intentions, I shall not refrain from distinguishing analytically between the constituent components of the categories that he employs.

97 Putnam, *Reason, Truth and History*, p. 49.

rather than entities. Moreover, there is no suggestion that the number of such potentialities is fixed.

The second component of Putnam's metaphysical realism is the idea that "there is exactly one true and complete description of 'the way the world is'."[98] Bhaskar does think that the aim of science is to identify the real essences of phenomena at increasing levels of depth. And if a given object has just one real essence, it would follow that it has just one real definition. Such a position would seem to suggest that Bhaskar also meets the second test for Putnam's metaphysical realism. However, Bhaskar quite pointedly insists that there is no absolutely certain knowledge and no complete description to be had. Rather, he maintains, all knowledge claims are fallible, and science is an open-ended process. In a similar vein, with respect to the issue of justification – which is what Putnam is really raising here – the question for Bhaskar is not so much whether one theory, considered on its own, is either perfectly true or perfectly false, but rather how one theory compares to another. It is the relative explanatory power of competing accounts that is assessed, not the absolute truth of a single theory.

Finally, the third component of metaphysical realism is the correspondence theory of truth. Bhaskar does not subscribe to the correspondence theory. Admittedly, one could argue that since Bhaskar believes (1) that there is a specifiable way that the world is and (2) that true theories tell us what this way is, he is a correspondence theorist whether he cares to admit it or not. Bhaskar himself, however, maintains that the correspondence theory of truth is unsatisfactory.[99] The upshot of all of this, it seems to me, is that the dichotomy between metaphysical and internal realism is not of much use in helping us to sort out what it is that Bhaskar and Putnam actually disagree about. To make any headway, we need to look more closely at Putnam's actual argument.

Putnam maintains that metaphysical realism is unintelligible. He develops two basic lines of reasoning in support of this claim, one having to do with language, the other having to do with conceptualized entities, or "objects." He also introduces an argument regarding

---

98 Ibid.
99 Bhaskar's attitude towards the correspondence theory has changed over the years. In *RTS* he rejects it outright, stating "There is no way in which we can look at the world and then at a sentence and ask whether they fit" (*RTS*, p. 249). In *Plato, Etc.*, meanwhile, the claim is not so much that the correspondence theory of truth is indefensible as that it captures only one of a number of different definitions of the concept, and an ultimately superficial one at that. See Chapter 4 for a fuller discussion of Bhaskar's account of truth.

the nature of causality. This argument is given less prominence than it might have been, but is nonetheless quite significant. Although the different lines of argument overlap and reinforce one another, the analysis of language is primarily directed at the second and third tenets of metaphysical realism as Putnam defines it. The discussion of objects, meanwhile, is primarily directed at the first tenet, although Putnam also brings it to bear on the other two. The argument regarding causality is primarily – though again not exclusively – directed toward the first tenet as well.

The crux of the argument based on language is there is no necessary connection between signs and that to which they refer.[100] In principle, Putnam tells us, any word could denote any object. Referring explicitly to Quine, Putnam writes: "[T]here are always infinitely many different interpretations of the predicates of a language which assign the 'correct' truth-values to the sentences in all possible worlds, *no matter how these 'correct' truth-values are singled out.*"[101] The well-known example from Chapter 2 of *Reason, Truth and History* (*RTH*) has to do with cats, mats, cherries and trees. "The cat is on the mat," Putnam argues, can be interpreted such that it is true if the cherries are on the tree. There is nothing about the word "cat" itself that leads it to refer to four-legged mammals who purr rather than to small spherical-shaped fruit with pits. This key point regarding the arbitrary, or accidental, character of the relationship between sign and referent is reiterated throughout Putnam's work on internal realism.

For Putnam, the fact that designation is a matter of convention, that meaning is not fixed by a property of signs, referents and/or the relationship between the two, is an indication that the correspondence theory of truth is unacceptable. It also tells against what he regards as the attendant conviction that there is exactly one true and complete theory of the world. The logic is as follows: correspondence is itself a reference relation. If it is the case that language attaches to the world only by convention, then the idea that there are or could be statements that are exempt from this – statements that do, somehow, attach necessarily to that to which they refer – must be mistaken. Truth cannot be defined in terms of a correspondence between sign and referent because the semantic components of language do not uniquely correspond to *any* given referents. As Putnam puts it,

100 Putnam, *Reason, Truth and History*, pp. 17–18.
101 Ibid., p. 35.

[it] is not that correspondences between words or concepts and other entities don't exist, but that *too many* correspondences exist. To pick out just *one* correspondence between words or mental signs and mind-independent things we would have already to have referential access to the mind-independent things.[102]

Similarly, it cannot be the case that there is only one true and complete theory, because to say that designation is fixed by convention is to say that, in principle, all the words of a given theory could be replaced with other words, without an accompanying change in the truth-value of the theory.

The discussion of entities, meanwhile, yields the claim that there is no meaningful way to talk about pre- or non-conceptualized objects. "'Objects' do not exist independently of conceptual schemes," Putnam writes. "*We* cut up the world into objects when we introduce one or another scheme of description."[103] And again, "The idea that 'object' has some sense which is independent of how we are counting objects and what we are counting as an 'object' in a given situation is an illusion."[104] It is important to capture the intended nuance of Putnam's position. As I understand him, Putnam does believe that reality includes mind-independent entities. It is just that it is impossible to specify what they are. Thus:

To deny, as I do, that there is a "ready-made-world" is not to say that we make up the world. I am not denying that there are geological facts which we did not make up. But I have long argued that to ask which facts are mind independent in the sense that nothing about them reflects our conceptual choices and which facts are "contributed by us" is to commit a "fallacy of division." . . . To try to divide the world into a part that is independent of us and a part that is contributed by us is an old temptation, but giving in to it leads to disaster every time.[105]

The thesis of "conceptual relativity" as Putnam calls it, is presented as though it were a direct alternative to the idea that "the world consists of some fixed totality of mind-independent objects."

102 Ibid., p. 73.
103 Ibid., p. 52.
104 Hilary Putnam, *Renewing Philosophy*, Cambridge, MA: Harvard University Press, 1992, p. 121.
105 Ibid., p. 58.

To my mind, however, it is not obvious what the logical connection is between conceptual relativity and ontological realism – and this because it is not in fact obvious what kind of a claim Putnam has made. Is conceptual relativity an ontological claim, to the effect that certain kinds of entities, namely, "mind-independent" ones, do not exist? Or is it an epistemic claim, to the effect that, regardless of what may or may not *exist* independently of our consciousness and intentions, it is in the nature of the case that anything that we can have *knowledge* of is mind-dependent? That Putnam is, at a minimum, committed to the latter, epistemic version of conceptual relativity is beyond dispute, I think. It is worth reiterating, however, that the epistemic version, as I'm calling it, of the thesis of conceptual relativity, is not an argument against the *existence* of anything. It is an argument, instead, about the limits of knowledge. Only the ontological interpretation of conceptual relativity – and only if it were persuasive – would actually tell against the first tenet of metaphysical realism as Putnam construes it.

The key question, then, is whether or not in saying "'Objects' do not exist independently of conceptual schemes" Putnam actually means to deny the existence of mind-independent entities. On this issue I think that Putnam is deeply torn. On the one hand, he clearly wants to say that there are things about the world that we did not conjure or imagine into existence and that we cannot will out of existence. Apart from numerous statements to this effect, such as the one quoted earlier, his realist inclinations are evidenced by, for example, his opposition to Nelson Goodman. Thus, writing about Goodman, among others, he asks:

> why should the fact that reality cannot be described independent of our descriptions lead us to suppose that there are only the descriptions? After all, according to our descriptions themselves, the word "quark" is one thing and a quark is quite a different thing.[106]

Putnam's belief in the existence of an extra-conceptual reality is also evidenced by the fundamental premise of the Brains-in-a-Vat argument, for which he is so well known. Although it is included in *RTH*, in which Putnam is otherwise concerned to undermine ontological realism – and although he periodically acts as though it *were* an argument against, if not ontological realism narrowly construed, then metaphysical realism as a whole – the point of the Brains-in-a-Vat argument is that reference is predicated on the existence of a non-discursive, or extra-conceptual, reality with which we interact. (For it is

---

106 Ibid., p. 122.

precisely by virtue of their world being absent of such entities that brains in a vat could not, according to Putnam, formulate in a meaningful way the question of whether or not they were brains in a vat.) Indeed, while the purpose of the argument may be to demonstrate that words do not have intrinsic meanings,[107] the Brains-in-a-Vat argument seems to me to be a forthright declaration of ontological realism on Putnam's part.[108] Putnam might reply that I've over-stated the case – that it doesn't follow from the fact that reference presupposes an extra-discursive reality that such a reality is *entirely* mind-independent. The bottom line, though, is that Putnam seems to be convinced that reality consists of more than our thoughts and intentions.

On the other hand, it is equally evident that Putnam wants to limit the significance of such an assertion. He allows for the existence of mind-independent entities (e.g., "geological facts which we did not make up") and/or for a degree of mind-independence of not-entirely-mind-independent entities, but he insists that such an admission is of little or no ontological import. Now, some of the reasons that he gives in defense of this conclusion are in fact misdirected arguments in support of what I've been calling the *epistemic* version of conceptual relativity; they are claims concerning what we can and cannot know and/or how we know. As such, they do not afford us any insight into whether or not Putnam intends conceptual realism to be interpreted ontologically. In qualifying his realism about those things that we do not simply "make up," he does, however, advance at least two genuinely ontological claims: one general, to the effect that "elements of what we call 'language' or 'mind' penetrate so deeply into what we call 'reality' that the very project of representing ourselves as being 'mappers' of something 'language-independent' is fatally compromised,"[109] one more pointed, namely, that the world is such that it does not include natural kinds.[110]

---

107 Thanks to an anonymous referee for this point.
108 There has been much discussion of the Brains-in-a-Vat argument; there are readers of Putnam who would disagree with my assessment of its ontological implications.
109 Putnam, *Realism with a Human Face*, p. 28.
110 Ian Hacking argues that Putnam's internal realism is best understood as being a combination of empirical realism and what Hacking calls transcendental nominalism. "The nominalist," Hacking writes, "does not deny that there is real stuff, existing independently of the mind. He denies only that it is naturally and intrinsically sorted in any particular way, independently of how we think about it" (Ian Hacking, *Representing and Intervening: Introductory Topics in the Philosophy of Natural Science*, Cambridge: Cambridge University Press, 1983, p. 108). While I agree with Hacking's characterization, I am more inclined than Hacking seems to be to take the position that he describes to be an ontological one.

The argument against natural kinds comes in several different forms. In Chapter 3 of *Reason, Truth and History* Putnam attributes the insight to Kant:

> I suggest that (as a first approximation) the way to read Kant is as saying that what Locke said about secondary qualities is true of *all* qualities – the simple ones, the primary ones, the secondary ones alike (indeed, there is little point of distinguishing them).[111]

Elsewhere, meanwhile, he talks about the issue in terms of the non-semantic character of the natural world. Arguing against the idea that causal connection fixes reference, he tells us that it is absurd to think that nature is "self-identifying." Thus:

> This is to repeat the claim that a relation can at one and the same time be a physical relation and have the dignity (the built in intentionality, in other words) of choosing its own name. Those who find such a story unintelligible (as I do) will not be helped by these declarations of faith.[112]

In addition, there is an argument about mereological sums: I am sitting on a chair, at a desk, on which rest a computer, several books and a lamp. "How many 'objects' exist in the world that I have described?" Putnam asks. We can add up the individual "items" – me, the desk, the computer, three books and a lamp – for a total of seven objects. But what is to say that the desk and the computer, for example, taken together, could not constitute yet another "object" – and so on.[113] This is, I think, at base intended as an ontological claim, to the effect that whatever it is that exists mind-independently either has no structure or is such that multiple, if not infinite, alternative structures may be correctly ascribed to it. I shall return to the question of natural kinds shortly, but for the present the point is this: insofar as conceptual relativity is construed as an ontological claim, it is not the existence *per se* of a mind-independent reality that is being denied, but rather the idea that any such reality has a determinate structure.

Finally, along with the arguments based on meaning and on the conceptual relativity of objects, Putnam gives us an argument against metaphysical realism that is based on an analysis of causality. Putnam

---

111 Putnam, *Reason, Truth and History*, pp. 60–61.
112 Putnam, *Realism with a Human Face*, p. 85.
113 See ibid., Chapter 6 and *Renewing Philosophy*, p. 120.

approaches the issue of causality indirectly, as a philosopher of language, rather than as a philosopher of science or metaphysics. Most often when he addresses the issue it is in order to argue that the relation of causality does not – cannot – provide signs with fixed referents. This line of analysis is intended to bolster what I called earlier the "argument from language." But he does sometimes come at the issue head-on. In "Is the Causal Structure of the Physical Itself Something Physical?"[114] Putnam contends that causality is not, in fact, usefully construed as "something physical." Predictably, Putnam himself maintains that the answer to the question raised by the title of the piece is "Neither 'yes' nor 'no.'" Nonetheless, he dismisses the idea that necessary connections are a function of the dispositional powers of entities[115] – the suggestion that "disposition talk," as he puts it, is not simply a pre-scientific obfuscation.[116] Instead, causality, for Putnam, would seem to be what the dominant, broadly Humean tradition says it is: a sequence of events rendered contingently predictable via a theory or "law" of nature.[117] As he puts it elsewhere, talking about counterfactuals:

> I think that what makes a counterfactual true is simply that the consequent follows from the antecedent together with various relevant natural laws or general truths, plus the initial and boundary conditions in those situations that it would be reasonable to regard as compatible with the intentions of the speaker who uttered the counterfactual.[118]

There is, however, a twist. In Putnam's view, causality has a "cognitive or 'intentional' dimension."[119] Specifically, while it may be the case that consequents follow antecedents regardless of the subjective concerns of human beings, there is no way to single out a particular antecedent as "the cause" of a given consequent without

---

114 Putnam, *Realism with a Human Face*, Chapter 5. Originally published in Peter A. French, Theodore E. Uehling, Jr and Howard K. Wettstein (eds), *Midwest Studies in Philosophy, vol. 9: Causation and Causal Theories*, Minneapolis: University of Minnesota Press, 1984.

115 I phrase it this way following Brian Ellis. In op. cit., *Scientific Essentialism*, Ellis defends a position that is similar in many ways to Bhaskar's. I believe that Ellis's defense of what he and Caroline Lierse call "dispositional realism" augments Bhaskar's transcendental realism.

116 Putnam, *Realism with a Human Face*, pp. 86–88.

117 Ellis, *Scientific Essentialism*, especially Chapters 6–8.

118 Putnam, *Renewing Philosophy*, p. 54.

119 Ibid., p. 57.

introducing the interests of the inquirer into the picture. To quote Putnam again:

> If we postulate a "non-Humean causation" in the physical world, then we are treating causation-as-bringing-about as something built into the physical universe itself: we are saying that the physical universe distinguishes between "bringers-about" and "background conditions." This seems incredible.[120]

Such determinations are made by *us*, Putnam maintains. In distinguishing between "background" and "cause," we make complex judgments about that which is thought to be normal in a given situation and about which exceptionalities ought to be regarded as significant. "Is all *this* supposed to be built into physical reality?" he asks.[121] The argument against metaphysical realism, then, is that because the distinction between "background" and "cause" is not a feature of the natural world, causality cannot be a mind-independent phenomenon.

The major differences between transcendental realism and internal realism should now be relatively easy to specify. First, Bhaskar consistently affirms the existence of mind-independent entities and processes. Moreover, he proposes that the "intransitive dimension" is stratified. Putnam affirms the existence of mind-independent entities and processes only intermittently; most often he maintains that such claims are unintelligible. To the extent that Putnam does grant the existence of a mind-independent reality, he seems to regard it as being without determinate form. Second, Bhaskar's view is that scientists produce knowledge claims the object of which is the natural world itself. This is the intransitive object of science, not to be confused with the accumulated conceptual resources that are necessarily brought to bear upon it in the process of inquiry. Putnam's view is that what we know is the-world-already-under-some-description; the world "itself" is not something to which we have cognitive access. Third, for Bhaskar, causality is the exercise of real dispositional powers. For Putnam, causality seems to be something like constant conjunction in conformity with the laws of nature, relative to an intentional subject. Fourth, affirmation of the existence of natural kinds is at the heart of transcendental realism. Central to internal realism, by sharp contrast, is the rejection of natural kinds. Finally, although a pronounced divergence of approach to the issue does not emerge until Bhaskar's later work, Bhaskar and Putnam disagree

120 Ibid., p. 87.
121 Putnam, *Realism with a Human Face*, p. 88.

about how best to conceptualize truth.[122] In *Dialectic*, Bhaskar advances a theory of what he calls "alethic truth." Putnam, meanwhile, conceives of truth as idealized rational acceptability.

Now that the actual differences between Bhaskar and Putnam are clear, I want to return to the original question of whether or not transcendental realism can withstand Putnam's critique of metaphysical realism. As in the encounter with Kant, I think that the answer is yes. At a minimum, a transcendental realist can (and to a certain extent Bhaskar himself does) offer a number of strong counter-responses, arguments that reveal significant weaknesses in Putnam's position. I shall begin with the substantive ontological issues of causality and the existence (or not) of natural kinds. I am not going to address directly the more general ontological disagreement. Putnam's half-hearted commitment to an external reality is good enough, and the concept of ontological depth can be incorporated into the discussion of causality. I shall then take up the epistemological dispute over whether or not the world "itself" can be an object of knowledge. Finally, although the differences between Bhaskar's and Putnam's accounts of truth are important, the concept of alethic truth is problematic enough on its own that I shall not pursue the comparison. I discuss alethic truth in detail in Chapter 4.

As I have already suggested, Putnam's views on causality are difficult to pin down. He rejects what he calls "metaphysical" necessity, but claims to believe in a non-scientific sense of "physical" necessity. In "Is Water Necessarily H_2O?"[123] he says that, in contrast to the empiricist A. J. Ayer, "I still accept a notion of *objective nonlogical modality*."[124] Indeed, he can even be read in that article as intimating that he supports "an *unrelativised* notion of physical possibility," as he puts it. In his most recent book, he again distances himself from Ayer, stressing "I do *not* think that 'bringing about' is a notion we can or should dispense with, or that causal claims do no more than subsume events under *regularities*."[125] In the end,

---

122 Arguably, the Bhaskar of RTS held an even more straightforwardly epistemic theory of truth than does Putnam. While Putnam insists that "truth cannot simply *be* rational acceptability" (*Reason, Truth and History*, p. 55), that it must "be identified with idealized justification, rather than with justification-on-present-evidence" (*Realism with a Human Face*, p. 115), the early Bhaskar seemed much more open to the idea that truth is simply rational acceptability to a qualified audience. See, e.g., RTS p. 249.

123 Putnam, *Realism with a Human Face*, Ch. 4.

124 Ibid., p. 70.

125 Hilary Putnam, *The Threefold Cord: Mind, Body, and the World (The John Dewey Essays in Philosophy, Number 5)*, New York: Columbia University Press, 1999, p. 146.

however, he invariably puts a phenomenological gloss on the concept of natural necessity,[126] and holds firm in his rejection of what he calls "non-Humean causality." The notion of "bringing about" that is retained is not that of the naturally occurring "bringers-about" dismissed in "Is the Causal Structure of the Physical Itself Something Physical?" but rather that of an intentional agent pursuing a course of action.[127] While all of this may appear to make Putnam a less challenging critic than would be a thinker who consistently and unmistakably holds to a non-realist view of causality, in fact what is interesting about Putnam is that he seems to recognize the weakness of a purely subjective account, yet to be unwilling to assert that causality is an inherent feature of the natural world. What does transcendental realism allow one to say to such an interlocutor?

For a transcendental realist, the first point to be made is that, as with transcendental idealism, Putnam's notion of causality cannot sustain an adequate account of the practice of scientific experimentation. While Putnam insists that causal claims do more than "subsume events under regularities," it is important to see that from his perspective it is not so much that they do something *other* than this – e.g., connect events to the exercise of real powers embedded in the physical world – as it is that they do something in *addition* to this – namely, necessarily express, or incorporate, the subjectivity of the person or persons who voice the claim. Those times when Putnam focuses exclusively on the phenomenon of "physical necessity" – a process that he does seem to think operates separate from our interests, and which certainly is an *element* of causality – it is hard to see that he is talking about anything other than constant conjunction.[128] Given that in this respect the Humean model remains integral to his account, Putnam is vulnerable to Bhaskar's charge that if causal laws were in fact grounded by regularities, then experimentation would be unintelligible.

Bhaskar's argument, again, is that causality and regularities – let alone causality and regularities the identification of which is

---

126 See, e.g., *Realism with a Human Face*, p. 89: "whether causation 'really exists' or not, it certainly exists in our 'life world.' What makes it real in a *phenomenological* sense is the possibility of asking, 'Is that really the cause?'"
127 Putnam, *The Threefold Cord*, p. 146.
128 Putnam himself is adamant that it makes no sense to resolve the concept of causality into a part that is "out there" and a part that we "project" onto reality (e.g., *Realism with a Human Face*, pp. 88–90). While I don't necessarily agree with his approach to these issues, it is not my intention to impose such a dichotomy onto Putnam's position. What I do want to do, however, is to home in on his concept of physical necessity. I think that this is fair.

inextricably tied to subjective interest – are ontologically distinct. If we assume on the contrary that causality *is* just the constant conjunction of events in accordance with a rule or rules – identifiable, in Putnam's version, only against a background of subjective interest – then we will not be able to explain why it is that the causal relationships that scientists discover by inducing regularities in artificially closed experimental environments seem to hold outside such environments – in particular, why they seem to hold even in situations where such regularities never normally occur.[129] Experimentation, Bhaskar insists, presupposes the existence of real generative mechanisms – i.e., "things endowed with causal powers"[130] – which give rise to manifest events, whether naturally occurring or artificially induced. One doesn't have to go as far as Bhaskar and claim that this line of argument points to the transcendental necessity of a realist conception of causality in order to maintain that such a conception has far more explanatory purchase than any non-realist alternative.[131] In short, Putnam's ultimate dismissal of the idea that physical reality contains things endowed with causal powers – "bringers-about," as he puts it – weakens rather than strengthens his position. Rather than capturing philosophically the latest developments in sub-atomic physics, it undermines his account of experimental practice.

Related to this first point, a transcendental realist would say that while Putnam appreciates that the production of a causal explanation involves work, he is mistaken about what the nature of that work is. Putnam focuses his attention on the distinction between background and cause. The physical world, he says, provides us with a multiplicity of actual causes for any given event. In developing an explanation, what we do is pick out just one of the many causes that an event has, and say that it alone is the "cause." All the other causes are then relegated to the status of "background." (And again: "*which* prior physical event we will cite as the 'cause,'" Putnam maintains, "is a context-sensitive matter,"[132] contingent upon our interests.) The work of formulating an explanation, then, consists of choosing which causes will be designated "background" and which will not.

---

129 Thanks to Hugh Lacey, for helping me to clarify my understanding of Bhaskar's argument.
130 Bhaskar, *RTS*, p. 49.
131 Thanks to Hugh Lacey for confirming this point. See, e.g., Ellis, who argues for what he calls a non-Humean metaphysic, very similar to that of transcendental realism, on the grounds of its greater "range" and "coherence" (Ellis, *Scientific Essentialism*, p. 262).
132 Putnam, *The Threefold Cord*, p. 146.

From a transcendental realist perspective, the weakness of this view is that, like Putnam's notion of physical necessity, it does not – and cannot, really – account for experimentation. On Putnam's model, the connections between an event and its many causes (Putnam seems to take it as an a priori principle that all events have multiple causes) are all equally necessary. The work to be done in producing an explanation is not, therefore, that of distinguishing between necessary and accidental connections. Rather it is a matter of deciding which predetermined necessary connection is of interest to one, given one's concerns. Setting aside the unaddressed question of how the multiple necessary connections between an event and its many causes come to be identified in the first place, the point here is that the decision-making that is at the heart of Putnam's model is unrelated to the process of experimentation. If the production of a causal explanation were as Putnam says it is, experimentation would be irrelevant.

Finally, from the perspective of transcendental realism, Putnam improperly conflates causality and explanation. While he is right to observe that we will get different answers depending upon what questions we ask – depending, for example, upon whether we are concerned with material cause or efficient cause, and/or upon the level of emergence with which we are concerned – it does not follow from this that the necessity of necessary connections is a function of our epistemic preoccupations. What Putnam has shown is that *explanation* is inherently intentional. And a transcendental realist would agree. One does not have to shy away from realism about causality in order to detail the ways in which knowledge production is intimately related to the interests – material as well as cognitive – of human subjects. But in showing that *explanation* is "context-sensitive," as he puts it, Putnam has hardly shown that the same is true of causality. From a transcendental realist perspective, all that Putnam has established when he claims, for example, that the "cause" of John's heart attack depends on the context of inquiry (either he ignored his doctor's orders to eat well and exercise or he had high blood pressure, depending on one's frame of reference)[133] is that different sorts of inquiry – in this case cardiology and psychology – have different object-domains, involving different sorts of causal mechanisms. We can even admit into the picture as richly variegated a conception of causality as Aristotle had, and say that whether we are concerned with, for example, formal cause or efficient cause, depends entirely on our practical and/or theoretical

133 Putnam, *Renewing Philosophy*, pp. 47–48.

proclivities. It still does not follow that the necessity of those connections that are deemed necessary is contingent upon the subjective
concerns of the inquirer. Even in the case of final cause – with respect
to which it does, in fact, make some sense to talk of causality being
inherently intentional (at least if the notion of "purpose" is interpreted subjectively) – it is the intentions of the actor(s) in question
that are regarded as causally determinate, not the conceptual framework of the inquirer.[134]

In his most recent book, Putnam himself says that "until quite
recently" he "found attractive" the view that "the notion of explanation has priority over the notion of causality." However, he now
thinks that the two are "interdependent"[135]: "the notions of explanation and causation presuppose one another at every point," he
writes, "neither has 'priority' in the sense of [one] being reducible to
the other."[136] It is hard to know exactly what Putnam means by this
latest pronouncement. At a minimum, I take two things from it. The
first is that Putnam recognizes that his earlier collapse of the concept
of causality into the concept of explanation is a weakness of internal
realism as he has heretofore articulated it. The second is that he still
does not treat causal processes in nature as ontologically autonomous
vis-à-vis human subjectivity. He no longer thinks that causality
reduces in some way to explanation, but he is not prepared to give up
the idea that causality *presupposes* explanation. The alternative
proposed by Bhaskar is that explanation presupposes causality, but
the reverse is not the case; the existence of causal mechanisms is not
contingent upon the possibility of their being explained.

At the deepest level, however, the disagreement between Bhaskar
and Putnam over causality is a disagreement regarding the existence
of natural kinds. Putnam, as I have already said, is opposed to the

134 This is not to suggest that an inquirer cannot have an effect on that which he or
    she is investigating. On the contrary, the social sciences especially must be
    rigorously self-reflexive. But while it is possible that a conceptual choice relating
    to how one explains event or structure x may itself bring about some event or
    structure y, or even effect a subsequent change in x, in such a case the explanation
    is the cause of y or x^1, not x. Also, it should be noted that final cause is not a part
    of the ontology that is developed in *RTS*. Bhaskar thinks that reasons are causes
    for behavior, but he does not think that they are the causes of the physical
    processes studied by natural scientists. Thus any talk of causality being
    intentional in the sense that reasons may themselves *be* causes is moot, for
    Bhaskar, with respect to the natural sciences. I shall pursue the issue of final
    cause, and its implications for realism, in the discussion of Bhaskar's philosophy
    of social science in Chapter 5.
135 Putnam, *The Threefold Cord*, p. 145.
136 Ibid., p. 137.

idea that nature is inherently and determinately structured. Bhaskar, by contrast, holds that entities are endowed with real essences, with reference to which they fall into natural kinds. Real essences are to be distinguished from nominal essences. A real essence is the "structures or constitutions in virtue of which [a] thing or substance tends to behave the way it does."[137] Nominal essences, meanwhile, are "those properties the manifestation of which are necessary for the thing to be correctly identified as one of a certain type."[138] Nominal essences have to do with taxonomic criteria; real essences have to do with the dispositional properties that account for necessary connections. I am not going to restate Bhaskar's positive argument for the existence of natural kinds based on real essences, set out in Chapter 1, although I will reiterate the appeal of it, which is that it explains, better than does the empirical realist alternative, a number of important phenomena, including experiments, induction, laws and the logic of scientific development. Instead, I want to focus on what I see as the flaw in Putnam's reasoning about this issue.

The weakness of Putnam's case against natural kinds is that it is based on a *non sequitur*. Putnam begins with the idea that the relationship between words and the natural world is conventional. Words do not attach to their referents with any necessity; nature, conversely, "has no semantic preferences."[139] The same is true of signs such as nominal essences. Like individual words, conceptual categories are social products. This first step in the argument is not especially controversial. Bhaskar, certainly, would agree with Putnam on the basic point – though, ironically enough, he is more careful than is Putnam to point out that, precisely by *virtue* of their social-historical character, the meanings of signs are relatively entrenched.[140] It is Putnam's next step that poses a problem. To get to the conclusion that there are no real essences (and by extension no natural kinds), Putnam must show that it either (a) follows from the claim that the natural world does not name itself, or (b) follows from the claim that the meanings of words are established conventionally. Neither inference is sound, however. The conclusion simply does not follow. At best, Putnam's repudiation of real essences rests on a reification of the linguistic conditions of knowledge, such that "We cannot make claims about the world except through the use of language, which itself attaches to individual referents only conventionally," is taken to mean "The world has no inherent determinate

137 Bhaskar, *RTS*, p. 209.
138 Ibid.
139 Putnam, *Realism with a Human Face*, p. 83.
140 See Bhaskar, *RTS*, p. 211.

structure." At worst, it is a dogmatically asserted and considerably revised version of Kant's view that there is an unknowable material "something" which exists independently of consciousness[141] – a version in which it is now possible to know that the "something" has no inherent structure. In either case, the objection stands: it does not follow from the conventional nature of *nominal* essences that *real* essences do not exist.[142]

Putnam, no doubt, would respond by saying that there is no way even to designate a supposed natural kind without recourse to language, to categories that are necessarily connected to human consciousness and intentionality. Curiously, though, in a rejoinder to Nelson Goodman, Putnam offers an argument against "world-making" that is very close to an argument that Michael Devitt advances against Putnam himself. Putnam's response to Goodman is that it is only those objects that are designated by proper names – such as "the Big Dipper," to stick with Putnam's example – that can be said to be *constituted* in some way by their names. Objects that are designated by general names, by contrast, such as "star," are, independent of their names, ontologically such that a proposed name either is or is not applicable. It is worth quoting Putnam at length here. He writes:

> Not only didn't we make Sirius a star in the sense in which a carpenter makes a table, *we didn't make it a star.* Our ancestors and our contemporaries (including astrophysicists), in shaping and creating our language, created the concept *star*, with its partly conventional boundaries, with its partly indeterminate boundaries, and so on. And that concept *applies* to Sirius. The fact that the concept *star* has conventional elements doesn't mean that *we* make it the case that the concept applies to any particular thing, in the way in which we made it the case that the concept "Big Dipper" applies to a particular group of stars.[143]

Devitt puts forward a very similar argument, but directs it towards both Putnam and Goodman: we can choose "which kinds we shall

---

141 See, e.g., Theodor W. Adorno, *Kant's Critique of Pure Reason* (ed. Rolf Tiedemann), Stanford, CA: Stanford University Press, 2001 for a particularly incisive treatment of this point.
142 Putnam sometimes says that the very question of whether the natural world has an inherent structure, independent of our account(s) of it, is meaningless. This is potentially a different line of argument from the one that I have just reviewed. The problem is that Putnam tends to present it fairly enigmatically, and offers little to defend it.
143 Putnam, *Renewing Philosophy*, p. 114.

pick out with words," Devitt maintains, but not "which kinds objects are members of."[144] What Putnam seems not to appreciate is that this argument – his own argument – establishes not just that the objects designated by general names *exist*, but that they have properties not of our choosing. One could, of course, respond that in establishing taxonomic and explanatory categories we selectively determine which features of the world we may eventually come to know. Surely in this way, at least, the identification of natural kinds cannot be separated from the pursuit of human interests. But in such a response we have shifted the terms of the discussion. We are no longer talking about whether or not the natural world is inherently and determinately structured, but rather about one of the ways in which science is necessarily value-laden. That we choose to gain insight into certain processes and not into others is a terribly important fact about science, but it does not imply that there are no real essences.

Interestingly, Nicholas Jolley notes that Leibniz charges Locke, the author of the distinction between nominal and real essences, with having made exactly the mistake that I believe Putnam to have made. Quoting Leibniz – "I confess, Sir, that there are few places where I have less understood the force of your argument than here, and this distresses me. If men disagree in the name, does that change the things themselves . . .?"[145] – Jolley writes: "Leibniz is surely right to accuse Locke of a gross [error] here. The fact that some people may mean different things when they talk of gold has no tendency to show that gold is not a natural kind."[146] Unlike Putnam, Locke did not maintain that there are no real essences. Locke believed that real essences exist, but that in the case of "substances," as he calls material objects, they cannot be known.[147] Still, the reference to Locke is worth pursuing, as Bhaskar has obviously appropriated Locke's categories.

Locke himself defines the idea of a real essence as follows:

> By this real essence, I mean that real constitution of anything which is the foundation of all those properties that are combined

144 Michael Devitt, *Realism and Truth*, 2nd edn, Princeton, NJ: Princeton University Press, 1991, p. 245.
145 Gottfried Wilhelm Leibniz, *New Essays in Human Understanding*, III, iii; A VI. 6; cited in Nicholas Jolley, *Leibniz and Locke: A Study of the New Essays on Human Understanding*, Oxford: Clarendon Press, 1984, pp. 149–50.
146 Jolley, *Leibniz and Locke*, p. 150.
147 John Locke, *An Essay Concerning Human Understanding* (abridged and with Notes by A. S. Pringle-Pattison), Hertfordshire: Wordsworth Editions Limited, 1998, Book III, Ch. 6, 9.

in, and are constantly found to co-exist with the nominal essence; that particular constitution which everything has within itself, without any relation to anything without it.[148]

By nominal essence, meanwhile, Locke says he means "the abstract idea [of a thing] to which the general name is annexed."[149] He illustrates the distinction with the example of gold. "The nominal essence of gold," he writes,

> is that complex idea the word gold stands for, let it be, for instance, a body yellow, of a certain weight, malleable, fusible, and fixed. But the real essence is the constitution of the insensible parts of that body, on which those qualities and all the other properties of gold depend.[150]

In the case of entities that are themselves abstract, Locke says, the nominal and the real essence of an object coincide; to know the nominal essence is to know the real essence. In the case of material objects, by contrast, the nominal and real essences are "always quite different."[151] In the latter case, real essences cannot be known. Locke is adamant about this. As Irving Copi observes, Locke's conviction in this regard follows from his theory of knowledge – specifically, from his belief that knowledge is ultimately of ideas rather than of material things.[152] As Locke puts it, "Since the mind, in all its thoughts and reasonings, hath no other immediate object but its own ideas, which it alone does or can contemplate, it is evident that our knowledge is only conversant about them."[153] Since we can have no knowledge of real essences, Locke argues, any sorting of material objects into kinds is necessarily done on the basis of knowledge that we do have – more or less by definition – namely, that of *nominal* essences. Those who claim to have sorted objects into kinds on the basis of their real essences, i.e., into natural kinds, simply have not done so; "that which is done by this attempt," Locke says, "is only to put the name

148 Ibid., Book III, Ch. 6, 6.
149 Ibid., Book III, Ch. 3, 18; Book III, Ch. 6, 2.
150 Ibid., Book III, Ch. 6, 2.
151 Ibid., Book III, Ch. 3, 18.
152 Irving M. Copi, "Essence and Accident," in Stephen P. Schwartz (ed.), *Naming, Necessity and Natural Kinds*, Ithaca, NY: Cornell University Press, 1977, p. 186. The article originally appeared in *The Journal of Philosophy*, LI (November 11, 1954), 706–719.
153 Locke, *An Essay Concerning Human Understanding*, Book IV, Ch. 1, 1; Book IV, Ch. 2, 1.

or sound in the place and stead of the thing having that real essence, without knowing what the real essence is."[154]

Bringing Locke into the foreground allows us to put the differences between Bhaskar and Putnam regarding natural kinds into context. Bhaskar is involved in an overt attempt to recover Locke's concept of a real essence. The concept is rendered moot by Locke on epistemological grounds, but as Copi suggests, there is in fact no compelling reason to decide with Locke that the internal constitutions of things are unknowable.[155] Locke himself writes almost wistfully that if we *could* have knowledge of real essences, such knowledge would no doubt allow us to explain those qualities of objects which form the basis of what limited knowledge of the world we do have.[156] Bhaskar's claim is that this is precisely what scientific explanations *do* allow us to do, and in just the way that Locke imagines. Thus Bhaskar writes, "There is no conflict between explanatory and taxonomic knowledge. Rather, at the limit they meet in the notion of the real essences of the natural kinds, whose tendencies are described in statements of causal laws."[157] Moreover, he contends, it is only if we conceptualize scientific explanations in this way, as yielding real definitions of real essences, that we are able to make sense of scientific practice. Putnam, by contrast, proceeds along the dominant post-Lockean trajectory, in which even the existence of real essences is eventually denied. Incidentally, although he is hardly alone in this, Putnam can be seen as ontologizing Locke's epistemological proscriptions concerning real essences in much the same way as he ontologizes Kant's claim that we cannot know things-in-themselves. However, viewed in relation to Locke, we can also see that Putnam's views do not represent the logical end-point of the trajectory; Putnam rejects real essences as the basis for natural kinds, but he is not prepared, as others have been, to affirm that language constitutes the ultimate ontological ground.

The final point of contention between Bhaskar and Putnam that I want to comment upon is epistemological rather than ontological.

---

154 Ibid., Book III, Ch. 6, 48.

155 As noted above, Copi thinks that Locke's conclusion in this regard is based on his erroneous view that it is only ideas that admit of (certain) knowledge. Bhaskar agrees that Locke's conclusion is "philosophical" rather than "scientific," as Bhaskar puts it (*RTS*, p. 60), but traces Locke's "mistake" (*RTS*, p. 60) to what he argues is Locke's necessarily ahistorical conception knowledge, namely, as arising from the perceptions of individuals, outside the context of social practice.

156 Locke, *An Essay Concerning Human Understanding*, Book IV, Ch. 3, 25; Book IV, Ch. 6.

157 Bhaskar, *RTS*, p. 174.

The question here is, "Given the mediated character of our knowledge of the world, what is it possible for us to have knowledge *of*?" To begin, it is important to recognize that with regard to the epistemic conditions in which we necessarily find ourselves, Bhaskar and Putnam do not actually disagree. Bhaskar is as quick as Putnam is to acknowledge that when we offer an explanation, we are doing something other than pointing to an object. If anything, Bhaskar is even more aware than Putnam is of not just the conceptual character of scientific explanations, but their social and historical characteristics as well. The difference between Bhaskar and Putnam on this point, then, is not that Bhaskar believes in unmediated cognitive access to the natural world while Putnam does not. Rather, it lies in the significance that each attaches to the mediation which both acknowledge.

For Putnam, the fact that scientists' cognitive access to the world is mediated by, among other things, language, mathematics and a preferred explanatory framework, implies that we may not understand ourselves to have knowledge of the world as it is in a pre- or non-conceptualized state. Putnam would have it that such a conclusion is unexceptional. It does not mean that theories are the only things that exist, or even that natural processes are "hidden or noumenal," he writes. Rather, he maintains, "it simply means that you can't describe the world without describing it."[158] But there is more to it than this. Barring the occasional disclaimer, what Putnam repeatedly tells us is not that we know the world, under some description, but rather that what we know is "the-world-under-some-description." To put it differently, the claim is not, in fact, merely that we can't know things without knowing them. Rather, it is that the act of knowing and the nature of that which is known cannot be analytically distinguished. Such a claim leaves Putnam in a very different position, I think, from that in which he presents himself as being in passages such as the one I've just cited. At the very least, by holding that we cannot have knowledge of preconceptualized phenomena, and yet maintaining that such phenomena do exist, if only in an indeterminate state, Putnam most certainly *is* saying that something about the world is hidden or noumenal. Beyond this, however, I think Putnam really must be seen as advancing an ontological claim regarding the constitution of all possible objects of knowledge – namely, that they are necessarily concept-dependent – and not simply as voicing a truism about what is involved in the activity of thought. If Putnam did not at some level regard "the world" and "the-world-under-some-description" as qualitatively

158 Putnam, *Renewing Philosophy*, p. 123.

different kinds of object, he would not be so intent on convincing us that talk about knowledge of the former is unintelligible.

Bhaskar, by contrast, draws no ontological conclusions from the fact that knowledge is conceptually mediated. For Bhaskar, the obvious fact that we cannot produce knowledge of an object without conceptualizing it is worth noting because it provides a counter to the "ontic fallacy," which lies at the heart of positivism. Important though the point may be, however, it does not imply that it is our conceptualizing of things that determines what their properties are. Indeed, it is a central tenet of transcendental realism that the intransitive objects of natural science are what they are regardless of whether anyone even cares to conceptualize them. Putnam asks, "Why should one suppose that reality can be described independent of our descriptions?"[159] For a transcendental realist, this is the wrong question. Of course we can't describe things without describing them. Nonetheless our descriptions are descriptions *of* things. What matters is not whether or not it is possible to think about things without conceptualizing them, but whether or not our concepts have explanatory power vis-à-vis the intransitive object(s) of our thought.

Putnam, I think, would respond that the transcendental realist has simply adopted a pre-philosophical stance in relation to scientific theory. In persisting in talk of cognitive engagement with "intransitive objects," he would contend, the transcendental realist has entirely side-stepped the issue of mediation. After all, what can it mean to acknowledge that we know the world only through one or another conceptual lens, but to nonetheless maintain that what we know in such a manner is the world "itself," as it is apart from any cognitive endeavor on our part? Anyone who claims to know something about the world in and of itself, Putnam would say, has simply neglected to render explicit the theoretical framework within which his or her propositions may be intelligibly articulated; anyone who insists that such knowledge is possible cannot seriously have come to terms with the idea that we do not have unmediated access to our surroundings.

It is not obvious, however, that Putnam is entitled to the last word. From the perspective of transcendental realism, it is nonsensical to say that the act of conceptualizing something removes the phenomenon from us as an object of thought. For the transcendental realist, thought is a means – though certainly not the only means – through which we garner information. To say that because thought is thought, we do not – cannot – think about the world "itself" is, from

159 Ibid., p. 122.

this perspective, simply to reify our own subjective capacities: the fact that we can think is projected onto the world in the form of "thought-objects," which must be taken to be the only possible objects of thought. Such thought-objects then function as effective barriers to scientific knowledge of the world. The transcendental realist does not deny that thought involves conceptualization, or even that scientific "facts" are most often theory-specific. What he or she does deny is the idea that thought itself bars us from having knowledge of the world – and thus that scientific knowledge claims may not be taken to be claims about the world "itself."

Ironically enough it is Putnam who, in disavowing what Bhaskar would call a "philosophical ontology," ultimately preserves the ideal of pure, objective knowledge. Bhaskar distinguishes between scientific and philosophical ontologies. A scientific ontology he says, is a specific, substantive claim about the world. Scientific ontologies are modified, elaborated upon or discarded as part of the ongoing process of scientific investigation. A philosophical ontology, by contrast, is a general metaphysical framework. Unlike scientific ontologies, which are produced through theoretical-practical engagement with elements of the natural world, a philosophical ontology is produced through reflection on the conditions of possibility of a practice such as that of science itself.[160] In endorsing a kind of ultimate ontological neutrality,[161] it is in fact Putnam who returns to the notion of unmediated objectivity: the practice of science in general, now – as opposed to individual theories – is thought to presume nothing at all about the world "itself." By taking the practice of science to be compatible with all possible philosophical ontologies, it is the internal realist, rather than the transcendental realist, who appears to believe in a presuppositionless scientific practice.

Putnam might actually agree with such a characterization of his views. Certainly the position described is congruent with the overall thrust of his thinking. The practice of science assumes nothing about "the world itself," he would say, because "the world itself" is a meaningless concept. To repudiate metaphysics for *this* reason, we can imagine him continuing, hardly puts one in the corner with positivism. After all, the whole point of internal realism is that there

160 In Bhaskar's words, "the former [i.e., philosophical ontologies] delineating the *general categorial form* of the world presupposed by the nature of scientific (or other) activities, the latter [scientific ontologies] articulating the *specific contents* of the world, characterized as the intransitive ontic objects of specific epistemics or research inquiries." *Dialectic*, p. 107.

161 Albeit inconsistently, since he also seems to maintain as an ontological minimum that the world "itself" has no structure.

is no theory-free knowledge to be had. Bhaskar's response would be to say that it is not actually possible to side-step commitment to a philosophical ontology. "The philosophy of science," he writes, "abhors an ontological vacuum;"[162] those who claim to be operating without a metaphysics are merely operating with an implicit one. The implicit ontology of internal realism is that of empirical realism.[163] Ultimately, then, the dispute over what scientific theories are theories *of* (i.e., the world itself or some other entity) amounts to a dispute over whether or not empirical realism is an adequate philosophical ontology of science. Bhaskar, of course, believes himself to have shown that it is not – and I think that he is right about this.

Having looked now at the actual points of difference between internal realism and transcendental realism, I will reaffirm my contention that Putnam has not, in the end, demonstrated that a realist position such as Bhaskar's is unintelligible. Nevertheless, I think that Putnam's views ought to be taken seriously. While I would not draw the ontological conclusions that Putnam does from the fact that knowledge is both mediated and itself a mediator, I do think that the issue is under-theorized in the works of Bhaskar with which I am concerned. Let me end by saying that in my view Putnam should be read sympathetically by transcendental realists. Putnam is not, at heart, an anti-realist. Rather, he is a realist who appears to be sincerely grappling with the problem of the relationship between subject and object. While I do not believe him to have resolved the problem in a satisfactory manner, I do believe him to have fully appreciated its gravity. For this reason, he has something of value to contribute to transcendental realism.

162 Bhaskar, *RTS*, p. 40.
163 See, e.g., Bhaskar, *Scientific Realism and Human Emancipation*, pp. 5–9.

4 Alethic truth[164]

Having looked at Bhaskar's effort to vindicate ontology, as he has put it,[165] I want to turn my attention to the concept of truth. Bhaskar has not written a great deal on this topic, despite a concern to defend the idea that science progresses rationally. Although he came out against the correspondence theory of truth as early as *RTS* – implicitly endorsing an Althusserian-style epistemic, or consensus, theory – it was not until the early 1990s, with the publication of *Dialectic: The Pulse of Freedom* (hereafter *DPF*) and *Plato, Etc.* (hereafter *PE*), that Bhaskar explicitly put forward an alternative account of truth. Bhaskar's theory of truth is centered on the concept of "alethic truth," which he sees as the basis of what he calls the "truth tetrapolity." My aim in the present chapter is to take stock of this approach. I believe that Bhaskar's account of truth is of little help in theorizing what he terms rationality at the level of judgment: the concept of alethic truth is unsound, and the truth tetrapolity into which it is seen to fit is untenable.

The discussion falls into three sections. In the first section, I look very closely at the concept of alethic truth. I argue that there are three types of reason – ontological, epistemological and what I have called political – for judging the concept of alethic truth to be either incorrect or more trouble than it's worth. The ontological objection is that the equation of truth and states of affairs is improper; truth and states of affairs, while related, are not at all the same sort of thing. The epistemological objection is that the concept of alethic truth makes it seem as though important epistemic issues have been resolved, when in fact they have not been. The political objection is

---

164 This chapter appeared in slightly modified form in *Philosophy of the Social Sciences*, 30(3), September 2000. © Sage Publications, Inc.
165 Bhaskar, *PE*, p. 47.

that the concept of alethic truth makes it seem as though critical realism is a scientistic and absolutist theory of knowledge, when in fact it is not. In the second section, I consider the notion of the truth tetrapolity, into which Bhaskar would have alethic truth fit. Here I suggest that the tetrapolity is not, in fact, the dialectical whole that Bhaskar would seem to think it is – that it does not, indeed cannot, generate a theory of truth adequate to the demands of critical realism. Finally, in the third section, I propose an approach to truth that I believe sustains a far superior account of rationality at the level of judgment than that which is supported by Bhaskar's current thinking. The argument in this section proceeds hermeneutically. After setting out an alternative framework, I try to show how adopting such a framework allows one to express coherently what Bhaskar himself might have – or perhaps ought to have – meant to convey through the notion of a truth tetrapolity. This re-reading of Bhaskar from the perspective of an alternative position should not be mistaken for a rescue of the concept of alethic truth, however. Bhaskar's theory of truth is unsatisfactory, and must be rejected.

Alethic truth

With the publication of *DPF* and *PE*, Bhaskar turned his attention from Hume, and to a certain extent Kant, to Hegel. In *DPF* and *PE*, Bhaskar sought to transform critical realism into a fully dialectical philosophical system. Dialectical critical realism, as it quickly came to be called, is a comprehensive theoretical framework in which the category of absence is seen to lead to the necessity for, and possibility of, what Bhaskar has termed "eudaimonistic" society.[166] The realism about natural and social structures that Bhaskar advanced in *RTS* and *The Possibility of Naturalism* (*PON*) is seen as being part of the "prime (first) moment" of a "circuit of . . . links and relations" which forms a larger conceptual whole.[167] Also part of the "1M" aspect of dialectical critical realism is the notion of alethic truth. I do not intend to address dialectical critical realism as a whole. My analyis shall be confined to the concept of alethic truth.

Alethic truth, Bhaskar tells us, is

> a species of ontological truth constituting and following on the truth of, or real reason(s) for, or dialectical ground of, *things*, as

166 Ibid., p. 163.
167 Ibid., p. 249.

distinct from *propositions*, possible in virtue of the ontological stratification of the world and attainable in virtue of the dynamic character of science.[168]

Bhaskar speaks of alethic truth mainly in the context of describing scientific advance. Specifically, the concept of alethic truth is an elaboration of the Identification stage of the DREI(C) model of scientific practice set out in Bhaskar's earlier work.[169] On the DREI(C) model, an explanandum is Discovered, possible explanations are posited via Retroductive argument, competing accounts are Eliminated and an explanans, in the form of an underlying causal mechanism, is Identified (followed by necessary Corrections being made to the overall theoretical framework). "What characterizes the moment [of identification]?" asks Bhaskar. Nothing other than that "(s)cientists are prepared to *referentially detach* Sj, or some (transfactually efficacious) phenomena at it, as real reason Ri for, or, as I shall also say, the *alethic truth* of, Si or a set of phenomena at it."[170] Or again, as he puts it in *DPF*,

> [t]he scientific neophyte is from the beginning confronted with inter-subjectively established facts, which have become referentially detached. Her job is to discover the real reason or truth of these ontic entities, the Sj of Si. Starting life as a subjective hunch, it may become for her colleagues an empirical certainty. When its reality is established beyond a reasonable doubt, science now knows the reason for, or one could say the truth of, Si – the *alethic* or dialectical reason (dr´) of the phenomena it set out to explain.[171]

Alethic truths, then, are the underlying processes that both natural and social scientists seek to identify. To be the alethic truth (y) of x is to be the generative mechanism that gives rise to x. Moreover, just as, for any given alethic truth (y) of x, y is the underlying generative mechanism that causes x to be, alethic truth in general is the totality of real, causal powers that give rise to both actual and empirical events. One would not be off the mark here to think of a recon-

---

168 Ibid., p. 251.
169 Bhaskar, *Scientific Realism and Human Emancipation*, p. 68. Here the model is DREI. The DREI(C) formulation appears in *DPF*.
170 Bhaskar, *PE*, p. 25.
171 Bhaskar, *DPF*, p. 109.

figured yet recognizable Aristotelian conception of form. In Bhaskar's words,

> [i]n science, experimental praxis . . . enables fallible access to the generative mechanisms of nature. This is the true world of forms, which account in all their complex, manifold and mediated determinations for all the phenomena of what identity theorists are pleased to call the sensate (which, to stress, is a category mistake) and non-sensate world.[172]

To return to the initially cited definition of the term, alethic truth can be seen to be the "real reason for . . . things" precisely because alethic truths just *are*, literally, those underlying real essences, or powers, which constitute the domain of the Real, as Bhaskar called it in *RTS*. Similarly, alethic truth is "possible in virtue of ontological stratification" because, in Bhaskar's view, causality as such can only be accounted for via the presumption of depth. In so far as talk of alethic truth is talk of causal relationships, it too presupposes ontological depth. Finally, what it means to say that alethic truth is "attainable in virtue of the dynamic character of science" is that the goal of identifying causal powers at ever increasing depth presupposes just the model of scientific progress that Bhaskar has proposed.

What are we to make of this idea? Is truth indeed a predicate that may be properly attributed to "things," as Bhaskar would have it? My view is that the concept of alethic truth is deeply flawed. As previously stated, there are three different sorts of reason – ontological, epistemological and what I have called political – for reaching such a conclusion. I shall consider each in turn.

The ontology of alethic truth

The ontological objection is the most fundamental. Simply put, it is that Bhaskar was right to insist, as he did in his earlier work, that ideas are not to be mistaken for underlying real essences. From the perspective of *RTS*, truth – as essentially ideational an object as they come – belongs squarely on the epistemological side of an epistemology/ontology divide. Gravity, conversely, is no more the "truth" of the earth's orbit than it is its meaning, or an expression of its narrative logic. The terminology carries weight metaphorically, but not, for a materialist at least, metaphysically. To suggest otherwise is to fall prey to a form of absolute idealism in which ideas are taken to

172 Ibid., p. 164.

be an independent feature of the natural world rather than the contingent products of human subjectivity.[173]

Of course, such a claim on its own amounts to little more than a pronouncement of one's disagreement with Bhaskar. For it is precisely Bhaskar's contention that, in the case of alethic truth, the term "truth" does refer, presumably properly, to underlying causal mechanisms. Whether truth is or is not purely ideational, that is, is precisely the point of the dispute. And even this way of putting it could be construed as misleading, or at least prejudicial, as it posits in advance the existence of a definite property, truth, whose characteristics need only be correctly identified. A proponent of a deflationary theory of truth, for example, would balk at such a formulation.

How, then, is one to register the complaint that, by identifying truth with generative mechanisms, Bhaskar has committed the very category error that he so deftly diagnosed in his earlier works? Perhaps a way to proceed is to set aside the question "Is truth purely conceptual?" and ask instead "What sound reason(s) might there be, if any, to assume that truth is *not* purely conceptual, and to therefore regard as legitimate the use of the term to refer to generative mechanisms in nature and society?" Such an approach reveals the weakness of the case.

Two preliminary points must be made, however. The first is that a phenomenon is said to be an alethic truth if and only if it is *believed to be* the underlying cause of that of which it may be said to be the "truth." Given this condition, our understanding of alethic truth must be refined. Alethic truth must be seen to mean something like "What we call a real essence when we are confident that it has certain specified causal properties" – or, to use Bhaskar's terminology, "What a generative mechanism is called once it has been 'referentially detached', i.e., agreed upon as being the 'real reason' for some given phenomenon."[174] The revised definition is crucial in that it reveals the term to have a necessarily subjective sense, given by the stipulation "when we are confident." Alethic truth is thus an inherently equivocal concept, peculiar in that while it designates ontic phenomena, its use in any given instance requires that certain epistemic

---

173 This is not to say that human beings are not ourselves part of nature, or that our consciousness is not materially embodied, only that ideas do not inhere in natural processes, or exist independently of human subjects.

174 It is clear from the previously cited passages from *PE*, p. 25. and *DPF*, p. 109 that the condition of possibility of the referential detachment of a posited causal mechanism is a subjective one, namely, "[w]hen its reality is established beyond a reasonable doubt" (*DPF*, p. 109).

conditions have been satisfied, viz., that referential detachment has been achieved.

The second point is that while Bhaskar has claimed that alethic truth is a property of things – "no longer tied to language-use *per se*"[175] – he has not rejected the idea that other kinds of truth may properly pertain to the evaluation of propositions. In fact, he has attempted to incorporate most if not all of the major propositional approaches to truth[176] currently on offer into the concept of a truth tetrapolity. At issue, therefore, is not whether the term truth applies to propositions, for this has been settled, albeit in quite general terms, in the affirmative. Rather, it is whether the meaning of the term ought to be extended, such that truth may also be taken to specify real essences and the causal powers that they ground. If such a case cannot be made – and the onus here is on Bhaskar, since he is the one who wants to increase the number of objects, literally, to which truth may refer – then we will have to make do with the propositional version of truth, which I accept, and which Bhaskar accepts with the qualification that it is limited. On this model, truth is indeed purely ideational, by which I mean that it is a characteristic, or possible characteristic, of propositions,[177] rather than a causal power of entities. In terms of the typology of *RTS*, it is an epistemological rather than an ontological phenomenon, an object of the transitive rather than the intransitive dimension of science.

Let me return now to the question of whether there may be sound reasons to refer to generative mechanisms as truths. Here I will be brief: so far as I can tell, Bhaskar does not in fact provide us with *any* reasons, sound or otherwise, why it would be a good idea to do so. It is simply asserted that alethic truth is "the truth of or reason for things, people and phenomena generally (including in science most importantly causal structures and generative mechanisms), not propositions."[178] To be sure, one has the prerogative of defining one's terms however one likes, but definitional fiat is no substitute for a persuasive argument. Meanwhile, although little is offered to convince us to endorse the move in question, there are good grounds for rejecting it.

175 This phrase is part of the definition of ontological truth, of which alethic truth is a "special case" (*PE*, p. 64).
176 Thanks to Tobin Nellhaus for this way of putting this idea.
177 For a useful discussion within the analytic tradition of whether it is sentences, statements or propositions that should be taken to be truth bearers, see William P. Alston, *A Realist Conception of Truth*, Ithaca, NY: Cornell University Press, 1996, Chapter 1.
178 *PE*, p. 64.

We have determined that what Bhaskar means by the term alethic truth is something like "What we call the underlying cause of a given phenomenon x when we are confident that our beliefs about what has caused x are correct." The concept of alethic truth is thus an amalgam of the concepts of causality and – at what might be called a meta-definitional level – subjective certainty. Is there any chance that the meaning of the term is a whole that is greater than the sum of its parts? I don't think so. The extensional content of the term is exactly that of the term causal structure; to be the alethic truth of something just *is* to be its cause.[179] Moreover, while the concept of causality can be defined without recourse to the concept of alethic truth, the reverse is not the case. We begin with the concept of the causal power of a generative mechanism, and then, for the purpose of meeting certain philosophical objectives, rename it "alethic truth." Meanwhile, the epistemological sense of the term, important though it may be to acknowledge, is nothing other than a tautological stipulation regarding the epistemic conditions under which the term's denotative meaning may be employed. The term alethic truth itself tells us only, and only indirectly, that we must already have come to certain epistemic conclusions. Far from authorizing such judgments, it presupposes that they have already been made, on grounds that the concept of alethic truth does not itself specify. But if the concept of alethic truth adds nothing to the concept of a causal power – other than an *ex post facto* affirmation that scientists have indeed come to be confident that a particular theory correctly identifies the basis for the causal powers of a given structure or "thing" – then there would seem to be no pressing reason to adopt the revised terminology. It is redundant at best, clumsy and misleading at worst.

The awkwardness of substituting the term alethic truth for that of causal structure becomes evident if one attempts to follow through with the recommendation consistently. If the terms are regarded as being interchangeable, it follows that causal relationships may be said to be truthful relationships. But clearly the propositions "Planetary orbit is the result of gravity" and "The relationship between planetary orbit and gravity is a truthful one" are not equivalent in any meaningful way. To be sure, a proponent of Bhaskar's position would respond that the use of the word "truthful" here seems improper because it is: "truthful" in *this* sense conveys what Bhaskar terms the "normative-fiduciary" aspect of truth, while our present

---

179 There is some ambiguity regarding whether the alethic truth of x is x's own real essence or the real essence of that which, in virtue of it's own essence, gives rise to x.

concern is with the "alethic ontological" aspect. A similar rejoinder would be proffered in response to the complaint that, while the concept of truth as we normally think of it seems to be internally linked to a notion of falsehood, the concept of alethic truth appears to have no such contrary.[180] The problem with such a line of defense, however, is that it does not address the real objection, which is that as soon as one makes use of the term "truth," one means by it something other than what Bhaskar means by "alethic" truth. The proponent of the concept of alethic truth has said "I admit that it makes no sense when you try to use the word truth in the way that Bhaskar is proposing, but that's only because you aren't really using it in the way that Bhaskar is proposing." This tells us that the term has an extremely limited application. To be as cavalier about designation as the intelligible use of the term alethic truth demands is to presume that one may indeed make words mean so many different things, as Alice puts it to the Cheshire Cat.

Barring the introduction of a private language, then, in which the concept of truth, in the case of alethic truth, is disentangled from all of its established associations, we must reject the proposal that truth be regarded as referring to the causal properties of underlying structures. Truth, we must conclude, is a crucial component of the transitive dimension of science. But it is neither a part of, nor an appropriate name for, natural or social processes themselves.[181] Such a conclusion is entirely consistent with the principles of critical realism as they were developed in *RTS*. Indeed, from the perspective of *RTS*, one solid reason for a materialist to avoid referring to generative mechanisms as truth(s) is that to do otherwise is to reproduce the fundamental ontological error of idealism.

The epistemology of alethic truth

The epistemological problem with the concept of alethic truth is that, because Bhaskar treats it as being in a certain sense foundational – and because it's referred to as "truth" – it is easy to suppose that it

---

180 It is true that in *DPF*, e.g., p. 110, Bhaskar affirms that "in dialectical explanatory expositions . . . what is false (as well as necessary) is in the ontological order itself, not (merely) in the epistemological order." Perhaps this can be taken to be a reference to a concept of alethic falsity. Even so, with reference to ontological phenomena the language of truth and falsity makes sense, if it does, metaphorically rather than literally.

181 The case is somewhat more complex with respect to social life, where the intransitive domain is internally related to human subjectivity, but the conclusion is effectively the same.

constitutes a criterion of validity. Apart from being incorrect, such a supposition makes it seem as though difficult issues of justification and of theory choice have been resolved, when in fact they have not been. That such issues do, ultimately, remain outstanding is an indication of the weakness of the truth tetrapolity as an overall theoretical framework, a matter to which I shall return later.

Bhaskar tells us that science progresses as ever deeper levels of alethic truth are identified. As previously described, alethic truths emerge at the point at which scientists referentially detach some causal process, y, having achieved inter-subjective agreement that y is indeed the cause of x.[182] At the moment of detachment, "causal process y" becomes known as "alethic truth y" – or, more precisely, "alethic truth (y) of x." Now, the epistemic question is: On what grounds are scientists justified in reaching such an agreement? What is the criterion for concluding that theory A, viz, "y is the cause of x," is true rather than competing theories B or C?[183] Bhaskar says very little in response to this question. In *DPF*, for example, we find only that

> (i)n general a plurality of hypotheses will be considered (Feyerabend's moment) in a multiplicity of research programmes (Lakatos's moment) until all but one are . . . eliminated (Popper's moment)[184]

at the E, or Elimination stage in the DREI(C) model of scientific discovery. "This is the fallibilist absenting determination within the epistemically progressive movement in the dialectic of science," Bhaskar says.[185] Or again, in *PE*, we are told that "Rigorous tests, wherever possible, under experimentally closed conditions, lead to the Elimination of inadequate theories."[186] Bhaskar seems to be satisfied that scientists do, in the end, agree upon which theories are to be preferred – in fact one could charge him with underestimating

---

182 *DPF*, p. 109; *PE*, p. 64.
183 I do not mean to foreclose debate over the definition of truth in favor of the realist approach that I prefer. Neither do I mean to suggest an exact equivalence between the proposition "'x is the cause of y' is true" and the proposition "x is indeed the cause of y." Rather, I believe that from the perspective of critical realism, assent to the latter implies assent to the former. I have cast the discussion in terms of the former because I believe that to do so results in a more perspicuous presentation of the issues at hand.
184 Bhaskar, *DPF*, p. 109.
185 Ibid.
186 Bhaskar, *PE*, pp. 24–25.

the degree of controversy and dissent involved in the establishment of such conclusions – but, as alluded to at the outset of this discussion, he has never been much concerned to determine the grounds upon which such agreement might be based. The closest he comes is a brief passage in *RTS*, in which he remarks that

> [w]e can then allow, for example, that theory Ta is preferable to a theory Tb . . . if theory TA can explain under its descriptions almost all the phenomena . . . that TB can explain under its descriptions . . . plus some significant phenomena that TB cannot explain.[187]

As a substantive criterion of judgmental rationality, greater explanatory power is surely a start. But it is far from a fully developed account, and there is no discussion beyond this passing comment.

Bhaskar's inattention to the grounds for judging theories to be (fallibly) true invites two potential conclusions. First, one might infer from the lack of analysis that it is inter-subjective agreement itself that is the criterion of validity. From this perspective, a theory is to be regarded as true insofar as scientists, for whatever reason, agree that it is true. To a very real extent, this seems to be – or at least to have been at one time – Bhaskar's position. Thus, in a move that would account for his lack of interest in the question of validity, he insisted in *RTS* that scientists must be left to themselves to determine the epistemic grounds for their own inter-subjective conclusions. Indeed, in *RTS* Bhaskar states explicitly that

> [T]he judgement of the truth of a proposition is necessarily intrinsic to the science concerned. There is no way in which we can look at the world and then at a sentence and ask whether they fit. There is just the expression (of the world) in speech (or thought).[188]

Bhaskar seems to have moved from this position over the years, but it is worth noting by way of passing response that (a) if judgments of validity are implicit in the activity of science, then it is not clear why philosophers ought not to be permitted to reflect upon them, and (b) a claim to the effect that inter-subjective agreement itself confers validity is difficult to reconcile with Bhaskar's opposition to relativism in its standard form. Second, and of far greater concern for

187 Bhaskar, *RTS* p. 248.
188 Ibid., p. 249.

our present purposes, in the absence of an explicit discussion of the issues surrounding justification, one might be tempted to think that a theory may be judged to be true precisely insofar as it yields an alethic truth.

But this can't possibly be right. Let's be clear: as noted earlier, referential detachment is predicated upon an already-achieved epistemic state. Specifically, the referential detachment of y, for example, is predicated upon a (fallible) judgment that the proposition "y is the cause of x" is true – i.e., a belief that y is indeed the cause of x. It follows quite straightforwardly that neither the *proposition* "y is the alethic truth of x" nor the *state of affairs* of y's being the alethic truth of x may be the criterion according to which the validity of the proposition "y is the cause of x" is decided. The proposition "y is the alethic truth of x" cannot be the criterion because it presupposes, by definition, that such a criterion has already been applied, and that "y is the cause of x" has been found to be true. Similarly, while from the perspective of a correspondence theory of truth it might point to a *definition* of validity, the state of affairs of y's being the alethic truth of x cannot be the *criterion of the validity* of "y is the cause of x" because the inter-subjective agreement that y is the cause of x – and that, by extension, "y is the cause of x" is true – is precisely what is required in order for the relationship between y and x to come under the description of being an alethic truth in the first place. In short, because it presupposes that we have already assessed the validity of competing theories, alethic truth can be neither the basis for, nor the substance of, such assessments.

The epistemological issues associated with the term alethic truth can be linked back to Bhaskar's earlier work. From the beginning, there was the question of the relationship between ontological realism and rationality at the level of judgment. Despite Bhaskar's early claim that "there is no way in which we can look at the world and then at a sentence and ask whether they fit,"[189] there has been a presumption, I would argue, at least among readers of Bhaskar, that accepted scientific theories do achieve such a fit – and that accountability to the idea of such a fit is precisely what is meant by the notion of rationality at the level of judgment. Moreover, there has been a tendency to regard the principle of ontological realism as providing an anchor for, and as thereby authorizing, judgmental rationality so construed. According to this line of reasoning, it is possible to discriminate between competing theories on rational

189 Ibid.

grounds exactly because there is a real, intransitive domain, the dynamics of which may be more or less accurately identified by competing causal accounts.

Upon reflection, one can see that the concept of alethic truth has simply taken the place of the concept of an intransitive object, or domain more generally, in ostensibly authorizing theory choice. Substituting the concept of alethic truth for that of ontological realism only clouds the issue, however. Ontological realism was never an adequate anchor for theory choice. Granted, the fact that judgmental rationality was left largely untheorized within critical realism was not much of a concern to Bhaskar, for the reasons already mentioned. But if ontological realism was an insufficient anchor, at least the epistemic gap in the theory as a whole was evident. One had only to argue that it is legitimate to believe it to *be* a gap, that the issues of truth and justification are in fact properly of interest to critical realist philosophers. The trouble with the vocabulary of alethic truth, by contrast, is that, while it is equally inadequate as an account of judgmental rationality, it makes the need for such an account more difficult to see. In this regard, the earlier treatment, if not satisfactory, is at least preferable to that found in *DPF* and *PE*.

The politics of alethic truth

The third set of considerations that I want to raise I have termed political, rather than epistemological, although the issues in question are, strictly speaking, epistemic. The concern here is with preserving the fallibilist view of knowledge that Bhaskar has consistently defended. The problem is this: referring to causal mechanisms as truth(s) means that it is proper to regard scientific theories as being accounts *of* truth(s). Claiming for science that it gives us knowledge, not just of a real, intransitive domain, but of truth (which surely only the initiated can understand to mean merely the causal powers of natural and/or social mechanisms), makes it all the more likely that critical realism will be mistaken for a form of epistemological absolutism. Of course, the charge of absolutism can still be answered. In principle, one may be as much of a fallibilist about knowledge of alethic truth as one may be about knowledge of causal mechanisms. And as we have seen, the objects of such knowledge claims would be extensionally the same. But if critical realism can still be defended against misinterpretation, the job is once again made more difficult than it was, or than it needs to be, by the concept of alethic truth.

Bhaskar's earlier work presents a challenge to readers whose anti-absolutist sentiments about knowledge are tied to skepticism about the existence, and/or relevance, of an "objective" reality. For those who hold that knowledge is relative precisely because "reality" cannot be objective in any meaningful way, Bhaskar's insistence on ontological realism seemed to imply a positivist approach to knowledge. If there really is an "objective" world, after all, why shouldn't knowledge be a matter of organizing observation statements about it? The task of defending critical realism on this point was not terribly arduous, however. One had only to show that it is possible to be a realist with respect to underlying generative mechanisms, without being an empiricist and without thinking that our efforts to explain the workings of such mechanisms must be correct, and therefore immutable. Although the judgmental rationality upon which Bhaskar insisted was importantly under-theorized – and although, as a result, it may have sounded as though knowledge can be simply read off of "the facts" – upon reflection one could see without much difficulty that realism about ontological structures does not in fact imply any form of absolutism about knowledge claims.

Now, as I have said, the same is ultimately true of realism about alethic truth(s). Setting aside the host of complications with the term that I have laid out, insofar as alethic truths just are underlying causal powers, their status as real carries no special epistemological implications. The case, however, is no longer a relatively simple one to make. The defender of Bhaskar is now in the position of having to show that although alethic truths are themselves "true," our theories about them are not necessarily true. Indeed, something that we identify as an alethic truth may turn out not to be an alethic truth at all. The reasoning that is required is awkward and convoluted. Moreover, the view that science gives us not just knowledge, but knowledge of truth, has to be defended against the additional charge of scientism, as well as against that of absolutism. The defense, of course, is once again that the "truth" in question isn't *really* truth, in the normal sense of the word, but is rather another way of expressing the idea of a causal power. As soon as the concept of alethic truth is replaced with that of generative mechanism (or real essence), it is clear that the claim "Science gives us knowledge of truth" is really quite unexceptional. In the end, however, all of this leads to the inevitable, if rhetorical, question: What is to be gained by using the word "truth" to mean something entirely different than truth? I can see no potential achievement other than a widespread proliferation of misunderstanding, leading to ill-formed objections to critical realism.

The truth tetrapolity

Let me turn now to the "truth tetrapolity" into which Bhaskar places alethic truth. It is my contention that the truth tetrapolity is wanting, as a theory of truth, and that in a sense the problems stem from there. What dialectical critical realism needs in its place is a clearly formulated realist theory of truth, commensurate with the principles of judgmental rationality, epistemological relativism and ontological realism, as well as with the preservation of a meaningful distinction between cognitive norms and underlying causal mechanisms.

For the sake of efficiency, let me begin by reproducing Bhaskar's presentation of the truth tetrapolity in full. According to Bhaskar,

> [a]n adequate theory of truth must take into account the fact that it is a many-layered concept, in which there are four basic components: which I will nominate the *truth tetrapolity*:
>
> truth as *normative-fiduciary*, truth in the "trust me – act on it" sense . . . we can take its paradigmatic locutionary force here to be in inter-subjective communication;
>
> truth as *adequating*, as "warrantedly assertable", as epistemological, as relative in the transitive dimension;
>
> truth as *referential-expressive*, as a bipolar ontic-epistemic dual, and in this sense as absolute; and in the sense I have already introduced,
>
> the truth as *ontological*, no longer tied to language-use *per se* and in this sense objective and in the intransitive dimension, typically achievable when referential detachment . . . occurs; and a special case of which is
>
> truth as *alethic*, i.e. the truth of or reason for things, people and phenomena generally (including in science most importantly causal structures and generative mechanisms), not propositions. [190]

190 Bhaskar, *PE*, pp. 63–64.

In other words, in relation to a claim <p>, for example, a theory of truth must account for "truth" in the following multiple senses: (1) the speaker is trustworthy, (2) there are sound reasons for believing <p>, (3) <p> accurately describes a state of affairs p and – and here's where the requirements become more controversial – (4) the state of affairs p, including (4A) the cause(s) of p. Bhaskar believes that the truth tetrapolity allows us to grasp each of these purported senses of truth, and, moreover, to ground the more superficial, or provisional, aspects of the term in its proposed fundamental, alethic sense. The "dialectic of truth," as he puts it, is thus one in which "we go from subjective certainty to subjective facthood to objective truth to alethic truth."[191]

In my view, the entire conception of the truth tetrapolity, including the place within it of something called alethic truth, is confused. At the most basic level, the concept of alethic truth does not, and cannot, itself serve the function of integrating the elements of the truth tetrapolity in the way that Bhaskar seems to think it does. The concept of alethic truth does not relate the truth of propositions to the "truth" of things; rather, it designates such "truth"/things. The tetrapolity, in turn, is simply a list. The inclusion of ontological, and specifically alethic, truth tells us nothing other than that, in Bhaskar's view, there is an allowable definition of truth according to which causal powers are truth-bearers. Parenthetically, one might note that Bhaskar has already advanced this claim. Including ontological truth in a "truth tetrapolity" is no more an argument for the correctness of such a view than was the original assertion.

If, however, the truth tetrapolity is merely a list of different meanings, or possible meanings, of the term truth – one of which is "the causes of things" – then what *does* hold it together? What is the mediating term, if there is one, between the epistemological and ontological components of the tetrapolity, given that it cannot be alethic truth itself? Indeed, to put it differently yet again, what sense can be made of the claim that the "dialectic of truth" culminates in alethic truth?

Bhaskar himself seems to think that the alethic basis of epistemological truth is articulated in the following proposition:[192]

---

191 Ibid.
192 As Louis Irwin has pointed out, Bhaskar here seems to regard himself as offering a real, as opposed to formal, definition of (epistemological – especially referential-expressive) truth. (Louis Irwin, BHA: Re: Thoughts, bhaskar@lists.village.virginia.edu, January 22, 1999.)

Thus we have optimal grounding for believing that "water is blue is true" (and not just a local accident or subjective delusion) when we are in possession of the scientific explanation for it. Thus we can write

"water is blue" is true if (optimal grounding) we are in a position to causally explain it (T1)

or

"water is blue" is true if (next best grounding) we have good grounds for believing there is a scientific explanation for it (T2).

This contrasts favorably with the triviality of

"water is blue" is true if water is blue (T3).[193]

But there are problems with such an approach.

First, to confound matters, the proposed criteria are presented as though they were somehow a reformulation of the concept of alethic truth. This is plainly incorrect. What we see here are proposed criteria for judging propositions to be true, whereas the concept of alethic truth expresses the idea that causality is a matter of the exercise of dispositional powers, with the added approbation that underlying causal mechanisms may themselves properly be regarded as the "truths" of that which they effect.[194] Indeed, these criteria refer exclusively to the non-ontological components of the truth tetrapolity, and are unrelated to the claim that generative mechanisms are themselves a form of truth.

Second, these criteria constitute an epistemic theory of truth in the technical sense of the term. Epistemic theories define truth in terms of specified beliefs, or belief states, of specified persons. In the version offered here, to be true is to be explained by an accepted scientific theory. By definition, an epistemic theory cannot link, or synthesize, the ontological and epistemological components of Bhaskar's truth tetrapolity. Indeed, the approach set out is in fact an instance of what Bhaskar refers to as truth as "adequation." As such, it does not do justice to the view of scientific knowledge to which Bhaskar is otherwise committed. It is true that Bhaskar is a fallibilist about

193 Bhaskar, *PE*, p. 26. Bhaskar does not specify "iff" in these statements.
194 Thanks to Noah Efron for this point.

knowledge, including scientific knowledge. It is also true that in *RTS* he maintains that there is no way to inquire into, let alone determine, the relationship between theoretical statements and the reality to which they refer. Nonetheless, as his ontological realism generally – and his attachment to the concept of alethic truth specifically – belies, Bhaskar is also entirely convinced that there are determinate ways that things are – and are not – and that it is the aim of science to try to identify such real features of the world. Such a conception of knowledge surely requires a stronger theory of truth than that truth is what we mean when a certain group of people have certain things to say about a given proposition and/or state of affairs.

If, however, Bhaskar's account of what it means for a proposition to be true amounts to a version of truth as adequation, as warranted assertability, then we are back to where we started. It is not at all clear, that is, that the truth tetrapolity forms a dialectical whole, let alone a whole that is synthesized by, or rooted in, the concept of alethic truth. As I shall argue later, what is required is an account of truth that does, in fact, relate knowledge claims to real state of affairs, and in particular to underlying causal powers, grounded in the real essences of objects. Such a claim differs significantly from Bhaskar's suggestion that one form of truth, namely, ontological, and specifically alethic, is the ultimate ground for another form of truth, namely, what I have been calling "epistemological" truth (comprised of Bhaskar's truth-as-adequation and referential-expressive truths). Within the truth tetrapolity, it is the referential-expressive aspect of truth, rather than its so-called alethic aspect, that has the potential to be developed in this way.

Finally, by considering what it could possibly mean to even talk of grounding "epistemological truth" in "ontological truth," let me try to dispense with the concept of alethic truth one last time. The contention would seem to be that truth in its epistemological sense(s) is somehow anchored in, or deepened by, truth in its purported ontological sense – that is, that the sense of truth that is properly a predicate of propositions has the force that it does by virtue of the sense of truth that is properly a predicate of things.[195] Recall that the term alethic truth designates nothing other than a generative

---

195 This is *not* to say that those propositions that are (propositionally) true are (propositionally) true *by virtue of* the things that are (alethically) true being (alethically) true (although, as I shall argue later, something quite close to this is correct), but rather that the *meaning* of propositional, or epistemological, truth itself is somehow tied to the meaning of ontological, and specifically alethic, truth.

mechanism about which we have certain epistemic convictions. To avoid circularity, therefore, we must, in interpreting a claim that alethic truth grounds epistemological truth, bracket the cognitive sense of the term alethic truth; otherwise we will have merely been engaged in a circular operation of "grounding" epistemological truth in the fact of an epistemic judgment having already been made. Such an operation leaves us with nothing other than the fact of the extensional equivalence of alethic truth and real causal powers. And if we restate the original claim in light of this equivalence, what we have is a statement to the effect that the concept of (epistemological) truth is in some way rooted in, or authorized by, the domain of real causal powers. Now, the idea that the concept of truth in some sense invokes that to which statements refer is indeed what we're after, in my view. But such a claim in no way encompasses the idea that causal powers ought themselves to be regarded as truth-bearers, or that it is this purported form of "truth" that gives other forms of truth their epistemic purchase. The notion of alethic truth is irrelevant, in fact, to the view that truth is a concept that necessarily refers us to a referent.

And if it is a mistake to say that "epistemological truth" is grounded in "ontological truth," neither will it do to say that epistemological truth is grounded in ontic phenomena full stop (i.e., the intransitive domain, no longer referred to as "truth"). Indeed, it is difficult to see what such a claim would even mean, exactly. One idea would seem to be that something called "truth" can be read off of phenomena in much the same way as proponents of positivism believed that knowledge could be. Such a position would be at odds with critical realism, however, for it involves the simultaneous reduction, as Bhaskar himself might put it, of both truth and knowledge to being. The meaning of the term truth is here simply given by the intransitive objects of possible knowledge claims. Similarly, knowledge production is here construed as a matter of simply registering such "truths."

The other possibility is that talk of the intransitive ground of (epistemological) truth is a way of trying to bypass propositions altogether, of somehow trying to refer to objects without making statements about them. In the case of "'Water is blue' is true if we are in a position to causally explain it," for example, Bhaskar would be seen to be appealing directly, without recourse to propositions, to that state of affairs which causes water to be blue. (For only such an appeal would exempt the explanation from being simply yet another proposition, which may or may not itself be true.) Here I would say in response that, while there are undoubtedly certain areas of life in which our engagement with objects is non-propositional, the development of scientific theory is not one of them. In either possible interpretation, then, the claim that truth is grounded in things is an instance of what Bhaskar terms the ontic fallacy.

In summary, while it may be useful as a typology of conceivable definitions of the term, the truth tetrapolity does not hold up as a theoretical account in its own right. Bhaskar is right to try to relate the concept of truth to real features of the world, but the way in which he goes about it is unsuccessful. As I have tried to show, the truth tetrapolity tends to break down into either or both of a pair of contradictory alternatives: on the one hand, the approach leads us to equate the concept of truth with the belief-states of scientists – i.e., with scientific consensus regarding substantive explanations; on the other hand, it leads us to equate the concept of truth with the intransitive domain itself. Neither alternative is acceptable, and the production of such a contradiction is a sure sign of something having gone amiss.

Correspondence revisited: truth, knowledge, justification and being

As I see it, the elements of Bhaskar's truth tetrapolity can be syn-thesized neither by ontological "truth" nor by ontic phenomena generally, but rather by a particular type of correspondence theory. A fine example of the kind of approach that is called for is that which has recently been put forward by William P. Alston. In a work entitled *A Realist Conception of Truth* (1996), Alston advances a position that he calls – ironically enough – alethic realism. Alston's alethic realism is compatible with the core precepts of critical realism, and is helpful in relation to the concept of truth in a way that is quite similar to the manner in which Bhaskar's own thinking is helpful in relation to the concept of a causal account. Alston sums up his position as follows:

> (t)he basic point is this. What it takes to make a statement true on the realist conception is the actual obtaining of what is claimed to obtain in making that statement . . . This is a realist way of thinking of truth in that the truth maker is something that is objective *vis-à-vis* the truth bearer. It has to do with what the truth bearer is about, rather than with some "internal" or "intrinsic" feature of the truth bearer, such as its epistemic status, its place in a system of propositions, or the confidence with which it is held.[196]

196 Alston, *A Realist Conception of Truth*, pp. 7–8.

Or, more formally, "A statement (proposition, belief . . .) is true if and only if what the statement says to be the case actually is the case."[197]

Alston's realist conception of truth is qualified in two important ways. The first qualification is that being clear about the definition of truth is not the same as having settled on criteria of validity; questions about truth must be distinguished from questions about what Alston terms epistemology (i.e., justification). It is the fundamental error of epistemic theories of truth generally, according to Alston, that they collapse this crucial distinction. The second qualification is that one may hold the view that truth "has to do with the relation of a potential truth bearer to a reality beyond itself"[198] without being obliged to articulate a "robust" or "full-blown" correspondence theory, as Alston puts it.[199] In this respect the realist conception is a "minimalist" account of truth, compatible with, but not identical to, more ambitious formulations of correspondence. To quote Alston again,

> [w]hatever the best story is on the details of the correspondence relation, we can know in advance that . . . [t]he right kind of correspondence will obtain if and only if the same declarative sentence can be used to specify the contents of proposition and fact.[200]

The definition of truth that Alston defends is far from trivial, as it would seem that Bhaskar would think.[201] On the contrary, I would contend that truth so conceived is in fact a necessary precondition of rational critique, including scientific inquiry. The concept of truth may not tell us much – and I will want to return to this point later – but it is indispensable all the same. While the present discussion is not the place to develop this position in full, the basic claim is that certain – though by no means all – of our predicative practices are unintelligible minus a concept of things either being or not being (or being to some extent) as they are said to be. The argument here is not a pragmatic, or instrumental one, e.g., "Thinking of truth in this way suits our purposes, given the kinds of intellectual activities that we

197 Ibid., p. 5.
198 Ibid., p. 8.
199 Ibid., p. 32.
200 Ibid., p. 39.
201 The charge of the triviality of "p is true iff p" may have been directed to Tarski, but it is clear that Bhaskar is dismissive of correspondence theories in general.

value." Though thinking of truth along minimalist correspondence lines, may, indeed, suit our purposes, the philosophical point is that we cannot help but think of it along such lines. Consider for a moment the concept of falsity. What of the idea that a false proposition is one in relation to which things are *not* as they are stated to be? One would be hard-pressed, it seems to me, to come up with a notion of falsehood that better captures that which we intuitively understand to be the epistemic failing of false claims. And it is not just the negation of expressive-referential truth, to use Bhaskar's terminology, that refers us to the relation between potential truth bearers and a reality beyond themselves, but the negation of normative-fiduciary truth as well. For what else can we mean by the concept of deceit, other than that a speaker has intentionally said of what is, that it is not; and of what is not, that it is, to invoke the classic formulation?[202]

I said a moment ago that the concept of truth does not, or at least ought not, tell us much. Let me try to expand on this point. Alston distinguishes between truth and what he terms epistemology, or justification. I want to insist on a further distinction – one which will seem controversial to some, quite unexceptional to others – between truth and explanation, or knowledge. Truth, in my view, is best understood as being a formal, regulative norm, to the effect that a statement is true iff what is stated to be the case actually is the case. Despite being a transcendental condition of rational inquiry as such, however, such a norm tells us nothing at all about actual or potential states of affairs. Accordingly, it must not be conflated with substantive knowledge claims. Knowledge claims, as shall be discussed below, are always only provisional conjectures, to use the term preferred by Karl Popper.[203] At the same time, truth must also be distinguished from states of affairs themselves, as argued in the first section of this chapter. While the norm has an ontic component in the sense that it describes an ideal relationship between propositions and

202 "To say of what is that it is not, or of what is not that it is, is false, while to say of what is that it is, and of what is not that it is not, is true." Aristotle, *Metaphysics*, Bk. IV, Ch. 7, 1011b 27–28, in Richard McKeon (ed.), *The Basic Works of Aristotle*, New York: Random House, 1941, p. 749.

203 See, for example, *Conjectures and Refutations: The Growth of Scientific Knowledge*, New York: Routledge, 1989 and (ed. W. W. Bartley III), *Realism and The Aim of Science: From the Postscript to the Logic of Scientific Discovery*, New York: Routledge, 1983. As noted later, there is overlap between my views concerning the provisional character of knowledge and those of Popper.

states of affairs, this formal condition implies neither (a) that truth is a predicate of non-linguistic entities nor, to put it differently, (b) that non-linguistic entities such as causal powers ought themselves to be regarded as truth-bearers. At least within the idiom of critical realism – which is (or was), after all, a materialist philosophy of science – phrases like "the truth of the matter," or even "The truth shall set you free" must be acknowledged to be metaphors.[204] As ethically compelling as such language may be, to lose sight of its essentially metaphorical character – i.e., to claim the actual or potential real identity of truth and being – is to take up the mantle of absolute idealism. Finally, for the sake of precision it is worth noting that, while Bhaskar may be right that the existence of underlying generative mechanisms is a material condition of the intelligibility of scientific knowledge, and while it may also be the case that the existence of *some* reality, although not necessarily under a materialist description, is itself a material condition of the intelligibility of the concept of truth as I have defined it,[205] neither of these points (a) implies that reality *is* truth, or (b) ought to be mistaken for the view I have advanced, namely, that something like Alston's realist conception of truth is a *conceptual* precondition of rational critique in general, and of scientific inquiry in particular.[206]

Having defined truth in the way that I have, I want to propose further that there is no way to be certain that the conditions specified by the norm have ever been satisfied. Popper has advanced this same position on the basis of Hume's argument against induction. While a critical realist would not – and should not – be swayed by an appeal to Hume on this point, the conclusion that truth cannot be known with certainty to have been achieved also follows from an appreciation of the fact that there is no extra-cognitive standpoint from which to assess the relationship between scientific propositions and that to which they refer.[207] For the purposes of theoretical explanation, at least, access to phenomena is conceptually mediated such that, beyond the most basic of practical activities, there is simply no

---

204 While he does not necessarily share my views, my thinking on this point has benefited enormously from conversations with Doug Porpora. The term "idiom," as well as the example of the expression "The truth shall set you free," are attributable to him.

205 Thanks to Asher Horowitz for this way of thinking about this point.

206 As one of the referees for this manuscript put it, so-called alethic truths are truthmakers, not truth-bearers.

207 For an interesting recent discussion of this issue, see Douglas McDermid, "Pragmatism and Truth: The Comparison Objection to Correspondence," *The Review of Metaphysics*, 51 (June 1998), 775–811.

way to get out from under a regress of propositions.[208] The meta-theoretical implications of this situation are not terribly grave, however. Indeed, the meta-theory of truth that I have proposed is nothing other than a statement of what it *means* to be a fallibilist about knowledge. For how are we to understand fallibilism, except as the belief that the norm of truth may never be conclusively determined to have been met?

Knowledge claims, meanwhile, must not be taken to be true by definition. This will no doubt seem an outlandish claim to those who hold to any version of the idea that knowledge itself may be defined as a set of justified, true beliefs. However, I believe that in conflating the categories of truth and knowledge, more harm is done than good. If one identifies knowledge with truth, the result is that one must give up either (a) recourse to the concept of truth as a critical norm *vis-à-vis* knowledge, or (b) the idea that our explanations at any given time may or may not in fact be true, i.e., the commitment to fallibilism. In the first case, the concept of truth itself must be thought to change as knowledge changes; in the second case, knowledge must be thought to be immutable. Of course, nothing of what I have said should be taken to suggest that we are prohibited from establishing norms of justification or of scientificity; only that adherence to such norms does not constitute a definition of the term truth. Thus, from the perspective that I am proposing, Bhaskar's claim that <p> is true if we (or others) are in a position to explain it (or again, in less formulaic terms, "(w)hen we know *why* something is true our assumption *that* it is true is *grounded*, in a way in which it is not when we are only subjectively empirically certain of it"[209]) is an account, not of truth, but of justification (and perhaps of what sets scientific explanations, in particular, apart from the other sorts of beliefs that we hold).

208 The claim that I want to make here is perhaps less sweeping than it sounds. I do not mean to suggest that propositional, or representational, knowledge is the only kind of knowledge, or even that what might be called a propositional mode of engagement with the world is in any sense primary. Thus I regard my position as generally compatible with the kind of neo-Heideggerian stance adopted by Charles Taylor, for example, in "Rorty in the Epistemological Tradition" (Alan R. Malachowski (ed.), *Reading Rorty: Critical Responses to Philosophy and the Mirror of Nature (and Beyond)*, Oxford: Basil Blackwell, 1990). What I am suggesting, however, is that there are limited but important – and arguably inescapable – contexts in which we are, in practice, confronted with propositions which cannot be assessed except through other propositions.

209 *DPF*, p. 36.

Finally, as already suggested, the justification of scientific beliefs ought to be seen as necessarily provisional. We may identify criteria that we take to be good indicators of a theory's being true, but meeting such criteria does not establish with certainty that a theory is true. Strictly speaking, we simply cannot know with certainty whether a theory is or is not true; not only must the categories of truth and knowledge be pried apart, but we must accept that there is also a gap between truth and justification.[210] In saying this I am not endorsing Bhaskar's early pronouncement that "there is no way in which we can look at the world and then at a sentence and ask whether they fit"[211] – unless it is to be taken literally, as a comment on whether it is best to view sentences, in particular, as the paradigmatic instances of truth-bearers. On the contrary, there is in my view no way to side-step the question of whether or not the claims that we make about the world are true. The question must be asked. It may be – as I believe to be the case – a question that in principle cannot be answered with certainty. But to say that a question cannot be answered definitively is not to say that it cannot or should not be asked.

In the language of critical realism, the concept of truth with which I have been working is a component (along with the concepts of knowledge and justification) of the "transitive object of science." As such, it must be distinguished from the "intransitive object(s) of science." Although the concept of truth specifies, in formal terms, the defining features of a hypothetical, ideal relationship between one element of the transitive object (namely, knowledge claims) and elements of the intransitive object (namely, real causal processes), it has neither epistemic nor ontic content of its own. The concept of truth is purely formal, designating neither the totality of possible knowledge claims, nor the totality of causal relationships, but rather an indefeasible norm of rational critique. Truth so conceived leaves entirely intact the idea that there exists a real, "intransitive object of science," comprising generative mechanisms at increasing levels of depth, and the events to which they give rise. It also provides a basis for a claim to rationality at the level of judgment, as I shall argue later, albeit not a guarantee of absolute knowledge or certainty.

---

210 Here I suspect I am closer to Popper than to Alston. Alston separates the *definition* of truth from *criteria* of justification, but seems to believe that it is, or at least ought to be, possible to determine conclusively whether or not a given proposition is true.

211 Bhaskar, *RTS*, p. 249.

From this perspective, the concept of alethic truth may be seen to be a confused way of expressing two key ideas, neither of which amounts to a claim that physical or social structures are themselves truth bearers. The first idea is that, as Alston puts it, propositions are made true or not by virtue of the reality to which they refer. Critical realists ought to agree with such a principle, it seems to me. After all, the bottom line of such a position is that while we are free, in a sense, to think what we like, and while it is up to us to judge which of our theories are most likely to be true, whether a theory is in *fact* true is not, in the end, a matter that is contingent upon our preferences.[212] In Alston's words, we are in a position of epistemic "vulnerability to the outside world."[213] As he puts it,

> [i]n supposing that what we believe and assert is rendered true or false by whether what a belief or assertion is about is as the belief or assertion would have it be, we are acknowledging a liability to falsity that is, in a fundamental way, out of our control.[214]

This sentiment resonates deeply with the spirit of Bhaskar's concept of the epistemic fallacy, not to mention his later notion of the "primal squeeze on natural necessity."[215] The only mistake, as I have tried to show, is in actually identifying truth with the phenomena by virtue of which given claims are, if they are, made true.

The second idea is that, as Bhaskar has argued since *RTS*, to offer a scientific explanation of something is to identify the underlying causal mechanism that produces it. As previously suggested, however, such a principle must not be taken to tell us what truth is, but rather what science is. To collapse the categories leads either to a relativization of truth, or to an absolutization of scientific knowledge. In Bhaskar's case, the commitment to fallibilism rules out the latter alternative. Thus the identification of alethic truth(s) with the

---

212 Except perhaps indirectly, in those cases in which we are in a position to alter the reality in question, such that it comes to conform to the requirements of a given proposition. This is a crucial stipulation, especially in relation to the social sciences, but note that even in a case in which the underlying causal structures are subject to change as a result of human intervention, it is still conformity to (a now suitably altered) reality that accounts, or would account, for the truth of a given claim. Alston argues this point in terms of the realist conception of truth being perfectly compatible with idealism as a general metaphysical stance.

213 Alston, *A Realist Conception of Truth*, p. 264.

214 Ibid.

215 See *DPF*, esp. Ch. 2, *PE*, esp. Ch. 1.

best scientific account(s) on offer results in the loss of truth as a regulative ideal. Moreover, for Bhaskar, at the same time that the *de facto* effort to ground truth in knowledge leads to what might be termed an over-subjectification of truth, his simultaneous effort to ground truth in "things," and more specifically in the causes of things, amounts to a parallel reification, or over-objectification, of truth.

Unlike the concept of alethic truth, the realist conception of truth that I have described does provide for a way of integrating the elements of Bhaskar's truth tetrapolity into an over-arching theoretical account. Let us consider each element of the tetrapolity in turn. From the perspective for which I am plumping, "normative-fiduciary" truth implies a subjective, or psychological, commitment on the part of a speaker to the norm of truth as defined earlier. Truth as "adequation," meanwhile, must be understood as referring to issues of justification, rather than to the definition of truth itself. Justification, whether it is based on coherence, warranted assertability, pragmatic value or any other principle, is related to truth in that true theories may be thought to exhibit any or all such features. But the causal order is crucial: a theory may, if it does, meet justificatory standard x because it is true; it is not true because it meets such a standard. "Referential-expressive" truth just *is* an incipient realist conception of truth, poorly articulated. Finally, as previously discussed, ontological truth, including alethic truth, is an unfortunate formulation of a set of ideas concerning the nature of the world – i.e., that it is real and that is has ontological "depth" – and scientific knowledge thereof – i.e., that it consists not in the observation of empirical regularities but in the identification of real dispositional powers and the causal relationships to which they give rise. Alethic truth may thus be seen to be a reminder that (a) the reality by virtue of which propositions are, if they are, true or false is one that is both intransitive and stratified, and (b) for a claim about the world to be scientific, it must be an explanation – i.e., it must point to underlying causal mechanisms.

The realist conception of truth that I have presented does the necessary theoretical job of authorizing judgmental rationality, but it does so in a way that "grounds" knowledge in a transcendental norm rather than in the consensus of scientists and/or in the intransitive domain construed as "alethic truth." While it does not allow for certainty, it provides a formal basis for critique in that it permits – indeed enjoins – principled appeals to the regulative ideal of correspondence. The crucial difference between such a model and standard versions of the correspondence theory is that the appeal in this case is to an idea, rather than to "the facts."[216] On the face of it, neither the provisional character of knowledge claims, nor the foreclosure of their determination by Being, ought to pose any particular problem for critical realists. After all, Bhaskar has consistently argued for fallibilism and against the commitment of the ontic fallacy. If I am right, however, that amongst readers of Bhaskar, at least, there has been an unchecked belief that we can determine the truth of theories, i.e., justify them, via the features of the intransitive domain, then the implications of the subjective character of knowledge can be expected to be met with resistance. The challenge for critical realists is thus to abandon any residual aspirations to foundation building. Truth is a feature of the transitive dimension of science. Specifically, it is a formal concept that renders intelligible the deployment of substantive knowledge claims. It does not, however – and cannot – offer any automatic justification for such claims. In sum, there is no "ontological truth" from which "epistemological truth" derives its theoretical purchase. No degree of consensus amongst scientists that their best theory is correct, or that a given posited causal mechanism is real, can amount to anything other than an epistemic theory of truth; no insistence by philosophers on the "truth" of things can amount to anything other than a category mistake.

In a sense, Bhaskar's account of truth is an attempt to bridge the divide between subject and object that he took such pains to establish in *RTS*.[217] Having championed the claim that the transcendental condition of knowledge is not the synthetic operation of reason, but instead the existence and operation of independent causal mechanisms, Bhaskar was left with the task of relating the "transitive" to said "intransitive object of science." The problem with Bhaskar's approach is that, in the end, he has simply identified the two terms. Alethic truth just *is* the object: "including in science most importantly causal structures and generative mechanisms."[218] As I have tried to show, such a response amounts either to the introduction of a profoundly misleading neologism, namely "alethic truth," to refer to one of the two terms to be related (viz., the intransitive domain), or to the collapse of a dialectical relationship into one or the other of its

---

216 Douglas McDermid, cited earlier, argues that it is precisely this formulation that the comparison objection undoes. I disagree with him that a regulative norm must be able to be called upon as a practical criterion of judgment.

217 Thanks to Asher Horowitz for this way of thinking of it.

218 Bhaskar, *PE*, p. 64.

components. Bhaskar was right in *RTS* to distinguish between the transitive and the intransitive objects of science, and right to remind us later of their dialectical relation to one another. But it is the fact that knowledge is produced by real, embodied beings, in the context of real social and material relations with one another and with nature, not the identification of truth with being, that bridges the divide between subject and object.

5 Recovering Aristotle
Realism about causality and the social sciences

In the preceding chapters, I have suggested that what is most significant philosophically about Roy Bhaskar's account of scientific knowledge is its metaphysical core – specifically, the idea that causality inheres in what we call the natural, or physical, world. While there has been a fair amount of discussion amongst critical realists regarding the applicability of Bhaskar's thought to the social world, for the most part the focus has been on Bhaskar's substantive sociological claims and/or on the methodological issues specific to social science. My concern is more narrowly philosophical. The question for my purposes is whether or not realism about causality can be defended in relation to social as well as natural phenomena. I believe that it can be, although certain modifications to the account are required.

There has been some debate over this issue in critical realist circles, though it has not been far-reaching. This may be beginning to change, with the recent publication of several relevant articles and a transcript of a discussion involving Bhaskar, Harré and a number of others.[219] It is worth pointing out that in *The Possibility of Naturalism* (*PON*) Bhaskar himself did not formulate the philosophical task associated with the extension of transcendental realism beyond natural science in the way that I have. Instead, he undertook to

---

219 For example, Rom Harré and Roy Bhaskar, "How to Change Reality: Story vs. Structure – A Debate between Rom Harré and Roy Bhaskar," and Charles R. Varela, "The Ethogenics of Agency and Structure: A Metaphysical Problem," in Jose Lopez and Garry Potter (eds), *After Postmodernism: An Introduction to Critical Realism*, London: The Athlone Press, 2001; Charles R. Varela and Rom Harré, "Conflicting Varieties of Realism: Causal Powers and the Problems of Social Structure," *Journal for the Theory of Social Behavior*, 26(3); Paul Lewis, "Realism, Causality and the Problem of Social Structure," *Journal for the Theory of Social Behavior*, 30(3).

address a number of long-standing debates within the philosophy of social science – and to outline the parameters of a substantive sociology. To the best of my knowledge, the main figures within critical realist circles who have concerned themselves with the specific question that I have posed are Rom Harré, Charles Varela and Paul Lewis. The primary objective of the present chapter, therefore, is to advance the explicitly metaphysical discussion that is in my view necessary. Let me begin by reconstructing the basic components of Bhaskar's philosophy of social science as he sets it out in *PON*.

Critical naturalism and the TMSA

In *PON*, Bhaskar argues that explanations in the social sciences and in psychology can and should be of the same basic form as explanations in the natural sciences. Scientific laws in the natural sciences must be understood in non-Humean, non-Kantian terms, as describing the tendencies that things have to behave in specific ways. Things behave in the ways that they do by virtue of the powers that they bear essentially. Such powers, when exercised, are the underlying causal mechanisms that give rise to manifest events. The same is true of social and psychological events, Bhaskar says. Explanation in these areas of inquiry should be fundamentally the same as in the natural sciences. To explain a social or psychological phenomenon is – or should be – to identify the causal mechanism(s) by which it is produced.

Although he doesn't express it in quite these terms, Bhaskar's claim is that there are at least two basic kinds of causal mechanism in the social world: social structures and actions (themselves based on reasons). Bhaskar acknowledges that such mechanisms differ in certain respects from causal mechanisms in the natural world. Specifically:

1. Social structures, unlike natural structures, do not exist independently of the activities they govern.
2. Social structures, unlike natural structures, do not exist independently of the agents' conceptions of what they are doing in their activity.
3. Social structures, unlike natural structures, may be only relatively enduring (so that the tendencies they ground may not be universal in the sense of space-time invariant).[220]

220 Bhaskar, *PON*, p. 38.

Bhaskar devotes an entire chapter to the claim that reasons, like structures, have causal efficacy. However, the explicit comparison between causal mechanisms in the natural world and causal mechanisms in the social world is limited to those mechanisms that, according to Bhaskar, comprise the object domain of the social, as opposed to psychological, sciences. Such differences place "ontological limitations on a possible naturalism," says Bhaskar,[221] leading him to call his position in *PON* "critical" naturalism.

The relationship between social structures and individual agency is captured by what Bhaskar calls the Transformational Model of Social Activity (TMSA). In the TMSA, social structures and individuals are separated by what Bhaskar calls an "ontological hiatus."[222] Social structures and individuals are contingent upon each other existentially. Yet they are "different kinds of thing," as Bhaskar puts it.[223] Social structures are relationships *between* people, defined in terms of antecedently established positions.[224] They do not reduce to individuals, or to the properties of individuals. Nor are they groups. They are objective patterns of organization – conditions of the very *possibility* of individual action. As such, says Bhaskar, they constitute the Aristotelian material cause(s) of individual agency. I shall return to this characterization. For now let me simply note that there are really two different claims being made here. On the one hand, Bhaskar is trying to say that it is social structures that (as we shall see) are the *object* of transformational social activity. They are what individuals act upon qua specifically sociological actors. I take this to be the meaning of the reference to Aristotelian material causality. On the other hand, as other critical realists have emphasized, Bhaskar is also saying that social structures are efficacious in the sense that they delimit the range of actions that individuals are likely and/or able to carry out.[225]

221 Ibid.
222 Ibid., p. 37.
223 Ibid., p. 33.
224 Lewis, "Realism, Causality and the Problem of Social Structure," p. 250 and *passim*.
225 See Douglas V. Porpora, "Four Concepts of Social Structure," in Archer *et al.* (eds), *Critical Realism: Essential Readings*, London: Routledge, 1998, originally published in *Journal for the Theory of Social Behavior*, 19(2), 1989, and op. cit., Lewis, "Realism, Causality and the Problem of Social Structure." See also Danermark *et al.*, *Explaining Society: Critical Realism in the Social Sciences*, London: Routledge, 2002, especially Chapter 3, for an extended discussion of Bhaskar's conception of social structures as causal mechanisms.

Individuals, meanwhile, are represented in the TMSA as *repro-*ducing, although not – except in rare circumstances (e.g., in periods of dramatic, intentional social change) – as *pro*ducing the social structures which both enable and constrain their activity. In general, the reproduction of social structures is accidental; it is the non-intended consequence of behavior that is undertaken for other reasons. Most people, for example, do not go to work in the morning in order to reproduce the wage-relation, put money in their checking accounts in order to perpetuate the structures of international finance, or patronize Hollywood movies in order to reinforce compulsory heterosexuality. To be clear, it is only individuals who physically act, in Bhaskar's view. "The individualist truth that people are the only moving forces in history – in the sense that nothing happens behind their backs, that is, everything that happens, happens in and through their actions – must be retained," he writes.[226] At the same time, social structures bear upon individual action in the manner described above.

Bhaskar contrasts the TMSA with three other models of the relationship between structures and individuals. He dubs the alternatives "Weberian," "Durkheimian" and "dialectical," respectively. In the Weberian model, social structures are produced voluntaristically by individuals. Indeed, for the ontological individualist proponent of this model, it is not even clear that structures can be said to exist at all; society is simply the sum total of that which may be predicated of individuals. In the "Durkheimian" model, meanwhile, it is structures that fully determine, or constrain, individual agency. Finally, in the "dialectical" model – which Bhaskar attributes to Berger – structures and individuals are represented as being different aspects of a single causal process. From the perspective of the TMSA, the problem with the Weberian model is that it does not allow for structures to be counted as causal bearers (or even, ultimately, to exist). Conversely, the problem with the Durkheimian model is that is does not allow for *individuals* to be counted as causal bearers. The problem with the dialectical model, meanwhile, is that although it allows for both structures and individuals to be counted as causal bearers, it does not register the ontological gap between the two different kinds of entity. As Bhaskar puts it, "People and society are not . . . related 'dialectically.' They do not constitute two moments of the same process. Rather they refer to radically different kinds of thing."[227] Only in the TMSA are structures and individuals counted as equally legitimate, yet ontologically distinct, causal bearers.

---

226 Bhaskar, *PON*, p. 81.
227 Bhaskar, *Reclaiming Reality*, p. 76.

For Bhaskar, a sharp disciplinary divide follows from the onto-logical gap between structures and individual persons. Social science is – or ought to be – an account of the former; psychological science is an account of the latter. I want to quote Bhaskar at some length here, as this has been a somewhat controversial point of interpret-ation. Bhaskar writes:

> [t]he importance of distinguishing, in the most categorical way, between human action and the social structure will now be apparent. For the properties possessed by social forms may be very different from those possessed by the individuals upon whose activity they depend. For instance we can suppose without paradox or tension that purposefulness, intentionality and sometimes self-consciousness characterize human action, but not changes in the social structure. I want to distinguish sharply then between between the genesis of human actions . . . on the one hand, and . . . structures . . . on the other; and hence between the domains of the psychological and the social sciences.[228]

My reading of this aspect of Bhaskar's thinking is that it is motivated more by a concern to distinguish between social structures and groups than by any disciplinary parochialism. Still, it is not a step that I endorse. While it may make some sense to say that social scientists are primarily concerned with the causal properties of structures, and psychologists with the action of individuals, the TMSA itself shows that there must be considerable overlap between the two types of endeavor. From the perspective of the TMSA, a social scientist who has nothing to say about individual agency will not be able to explain how a social structure is reproduced. Conversely, a psychologist with nothing to say about the way that social structures delimit the range of choices that individuals have will not be able to fully understand why people act in the ways that they do. This said, I shall nonetheless follow the contours of Bhaskar's ontology in the discussion to come. I turn in the next section to a consideration of social structures and, in the final section, to an analysis of individual agency.

Before moving on, however, I want to make two further comments. The first has to do with Bhaskar's curious lack of attention to what we might want to call collective actors. Bhaskar's main concern with respect to groups is to stipulate that they are not what he means by the term social structure. Thus he writes,

228 Ibid., pp. 79–80.

[s]ociology is not concerned, as such, with large-scale, mass or group behavior (conceived as the behavior of large numbers, masses or groups of individuals). Rather it is concerned, at least paradigmatically, with the persistent *relations* between individuals (and groups), and with the relations between these relations (and between such relations and nature and the products of such relations).[229]

And again: "mass behavior is an interesting social-psychological phenomenon, but it is not the subject matter of sociology."[230] Just how Bhaskar does conceptualize groups is not completely clear in *PON*. At times he clearly sounds as though he thinks that group behavior is simply the behavior of large numbers of individuals. However, there is also textual evidence to show that he does not hold this view – that he himself sees groups in relational terms.[231] I am not going to argue the point either way. My purpose in raising the issue is to explain why I have not developed a separate discussion of collective actors. I have proceeded in the way that I have because (1) Bhaskar himself does not pursue the matter in *PON*, and (2) collective actors can be incorporated either into the discussion of structures or into the discussion of individuals, depending upon how they are conceptualized. While further analysis of groups would no doubt be of interest, it is not essential to the logic of the argument that I am trying to make. My own view is that collective actors should be understood in holist terms. However, as corporate entities I believe that they are more like structures than they are like individual persons. Consequently – as I shall argue is the case with respect to social relations – they are formal causes but not efficient causes, to use the Aristotelian terminology.

The second point that I want to make has to do with the link between critical realism and the TMSA. In my view, Bhaskar argues for the extension of transcendental realism to social reality in a circuitous and potentially misleading way. Alluding to Kant, he begins with the question "What properties do societies possess that might make them objects of knowledge?"[232] I interpret, or perhaps would prefer, this question to mean "What would society have to be like, in order for the model of science associated with transcendental

---

229 Bhaskar, *PON*, pp. 28–29.
230 Ibid., p. 29.
231 This interpretation was suggested to me by Howard Engelskirchen. Personal conversation, September 2002.
232 Bhaskar, *PON*, p. 25.

realism to be applicable to the study of it?" More or less by definition, the answer to this question is that as a condition of its applicability, a transcendental realist model of social science requires an object of study that (a) can be said to be intransitive, (b) is characterized by ontological depth and (c) contains causal mechanisms. The issue, then, is whether or not society – or any other social phenomenon – is such an object. Bhaskar answers that it is. The argument is that social structures are intransitive in the sense that they both pre-exist and are presupposed by the actions carried out by persons; they provide for ontological depth in that they are the not-directly-empirically-accessible generative mechanisms that give rise to manifest events; they are causal mechanisms in that they both enable and delimit intentional activity.

The point that I want to make is this: while the TMSA is a social theoretical framework that is *consistent* with transcendental realism, it is not an alternative formulation *of* transcendental realism. Let me put it this way: there are really two different questions that have been asked. The original question (as I interpreted it) is "What would society have to be like in order for transcendental realism to be applicable to the study of it?" The further question is "What *is* society like?" In my view, the TMSA must be seen to be an answer to the second question, rather than the first. It is but one theory of society – and more specifically of the relationship between social structures and individual actors – that is consistent with transcendental realism. To put it in the language of *RTS*, the TMSA is a scientific rather than a philosophical ontology. What this implies is that the soundness of critical naturalism is dependent upon the soundness of a substantive, if general, social scientific theory. The counter-argument to this claim is that Bhaskar's account of the relationship between structures and individuals is in fact a transcendental necessity of some feature of our experience, and therefore counts as a philosophical ontology as Bhaskar defines the term. This is indeed what some critical realists do affirm, but I believe that it is an unnecessary over-statement of the case.

Causal powers and social structures

As I have said, the question that is of interest for the purposes of the present discussion is not "Which causal mechanisms can be identified if one adopts a critical realist stance?" but rather "Can the claim that social structures are bearers of causal powers be defended philosophically?" I believe that the answer is yes. In trying to make good on this claim, I shall proceed as follows. I will begin with what debate there has been amongst critical realists. Here I shall be relatively brief. I will then move on to a more detailed analysis of the position on this matter taken by Brian Ellis. Ellis is the author of a theory of causality that is in many respects indistinguishable from Bhaskar's. Unlike Bhaskar, however, Ellis holds that dispositional realism, as he terms it, does not apply to social phenomena.

I have weighted the discussion in the way that I have for two reasons. The first is that there is a sense in which the objections put forward by those working within a critical realist framework can be responded to more easily than can those that come from Ellis. This is not to say that the former are any less serious or insightful than the latter. I would not want to be read as suggesting this. Rather, as Paul Lewis argues, there is a way in which the core "internal objection," as I shall call it, can be accommodated without undue difficulty by those who believe that realism about causality can meaningfully and properly be extended to social structures.[233] I am not sure that this is so with Ellis's work. The second reason to focus more closely on Ellis is that I believe that conversation between critical realists and philosophers from other backgrounds is sorely needed. While Ellis's views on metaphysics and philosophy of science hardly count as mainstream, as an interlocutor he nonetheless potentially opens up the discussion to a wider philosophical audience than Bhaskar's work has thus far reached.

The "internal" debate

Within critical realist circles, the main proponents of the view that realism about causality may not be extended to social structures are Rom Harré and Charles Varela. Harré and Varela argue, both jointly and independently, that social structures cannot be causal mechanisms. Social structures cannot be causal mechanisms, they say, because, as Varela puts it (following Harré and Madden), "causation is the activity of powerful particulars doing forceful work."[234] Social structures are incapable of doing forceful work. Therefore, they cannot be said to be powerful particulars. Powerful particulars are "singular structural unit[s] of activity," say Harré and Varela.[235] In the social world, it is only individuals that meet this criterion. The claim, then, is that realism about causality cannot be extended to

233 Lewis, "Realism, Causality and the Problem of Social Structure," pp. 264–265.
234 Varela, "The Ethogenics of Agency and Structure: A Metaphysical Problem," p. 65.
235 Varela and Rom Harré, "Conflicting Varieties of Realism: Causal Powers and the Problems of Social Structure," p. 322.

social structures because social structures are not in fact causally efficacious. To assign causal efficacy to social structures, Harré and Varela argue, one must first be prepared to de-couple the concepts of "power" and "particular," and then be willing to say that it is powers themselves that "activate" given particulars, including structures. The first step they dub the fallacy of bifurcation; the second they call the fallacy of activation. In their view, such an operation amounts to reifying the capacities of genuine powerful particulars (namely, people, in the case of social reality).

Harré and Varela augment their ontological assessment of social structures as construed by critical realists with a substantive socio-logical claim to the effect that what critical realists call social structures are better understood as ongoing, inter-subjective practices of story-telling.[236] From this perspective, so-called "structures" – such as class or feudalism, to use Harré's examples – are nothing other than abstractions. "Where we have to beware," Harré warns, "is if we start to treat diachronic processes, which are event sequences, as if they were synchronic entities."[237] Here the point is not just that social structures are not powerful particulars, but that, as conceived by critical realists, they do not actually exist. To quote Harré,

> Roy Bhaskar and Margaret Archer think that people are trapped in social structures. But if social structures don't exist in any interesting sense but are only taxonomic categories, then people can't be trapped in them. One can be trapped by a herd of elephants, but not by the species to which [the] word "elephant" as a classificatory category refers.[238]

In a recent article entitled "Realism, Causality and the Problem of Social Structure," Paul Lewis (2000) has intervened directly in this debate. Lewis argues that critical realists should acknowledge that social structures are not efficient causes. They are, however, he contends, material causes. Qua material causes, they have the effects previously described of both enabling certain behaviors and delimiting the range of options that are available to people. As Varela notes in a subsequent reply, Lewis underscores the temporal aspect of

---

236 Lewis discusses this well in "Realism, Causality and the Problem of Social Structure."

237 Harré, "How to Change Reality: Story vs. Structure – A Debate Between Rom Harré and Roy Bhaskar," p. 23.

238 Ibid., p. 26.

social structures.[239] Citing Marx's observation that we make history, but not under conditions of our own choosing, Lewis writes

> [p]re-existing social structures, the deposit or residue of actions undertaken in the past, provide the context in which current action takes place. As we have seen, these historically given structures condition (but do not determine) people's behavior in the present by laying down an initial distribution of resources and vested interests.[240]

Lewis recommends J. L. Mackie's concept of an "INUS condition" as a way of expressing the efficacy of material cause.[241] INUS stands for Insufficient but Necessary, Unnecessary but Sufficient. In Lewis's view, it captures well the idea that "social structure is a necessary but insufficient part of a causal complex that is sufficient but unnecessary for the occurrence of a particular social event."[242] Thus, for Lewis, individuals are powerful particulars, while social structures are INUS conditions.[243] Lewis argues further that Harré and Varela's subjectivist reconception of structure as conversation has limited explanatory potential. In particular, it does not allow us to understand the exercise of power. Varela, meanwhile, has responded that even a characterization of structures as material causes is a reification of human agency.[244]

In my view, Lewis is right to say that social structures as conceived by critical realists are not efficient causes. As has been well observed, Bhaskar himself claims that within the social world it is only people who have the capacity to initiate events. Given that Bhaskar holds such a view, it simply cannot be the case that "[he] has resurrected the Durkheimian premise that social structure is an efficient cause," as Varela would have it.[245] Indeed, Benton has charged Bhaskar with methodological individualism precisely because of his contention that it is only people who act.[246] The question for critical realists, then, is:

239 Charles R. Varela, "The Impossibility of Which Naturalism? A Response and Reply," *Journal for the Theory of Social Behavior*, 32(1), March 2002.
240 Lewis, "Realism, Causality and the Problem of Social Structure," p. 260.
241 Ibid., p. 264.
242 Ibid.
243 Ibid.
244 Varela, "The Impossibility of Which Naturalism: A Response and Reply," p. 110.
245 Ibid., p. 105.
246 Ted Benton, "Realism and Social Science: Some Comments on Roy Bhaskar's 'The Possibility of Naturalism,'" in Margaret Archer, Roy Bhaskar, Andrew Collier, Tony Lawson and Alan Norrie (eds), *Critical Realism: Essential Readings*.

if social structures are not bearers of efficient causality, what kind of causal bearers are they?

I think that Lewis is mistaken to think of social structures as material causes, at least *vis-à-vis* the actions of individuals. Admittedly, there is a sense in which the category of material causality is relevant. As noted, social structures may be said to be material causes in that they are that which is acted upon by individuals in the course of their ongoing reproduction of social life. However, this tells us that social structures are the material causes of *society*, not of agency as such. Material causality does not capture the sense in which social structures are thought by critical realists to be causally efficacious *vis-à-vis* individual action as such. As antecedently established relational positions that both enable and delimit potential courses of action, social structures are formal causes, not material causes.

Aristotle's typology, recall, involves four different kinds of causal relationship – or perhaps more accurately, four different senses of what we mean by causality:[247] material, formal, efficient, and final. Material cause, Aristotle says, refers to "that from which a thing is made and continues to be made – for example, the bronze of a statue."[248] Formal cause, by contrast, refers to "the form or pattern of a thing."[249] Efficient cause, meanwhile, refers to the "original source of change or rest."[250] Final cause refers to "the end," or purpose of a thing. "This is what something is for," says Aristotle, "as health, for example, may be what walking is for. If asked, 'Why is he walking?', we reply 'To get healthy', and in saying this we mean to explain the cause of his walking."[251] Formal, efficient and final causality are intimately related in Aristotle's metaphysics: form is thought to be a dynamic, inner force, the realization of which is the purpose of those changes that have been causally determined.[252]

I am not proposing that a fully Aristotelian notion of form-as-cause be adopted as a critical realist meta-theory of the efficacy of causal structures. At the most basic level, Bhaskar's concept of real

---

247 I owe this distinction to Jonathan Lear, who draws attention to the fact that "What [Aristotle] actually cites are not four causes, but four *fashions* in which we cite the cause" (Jonathan Lear, *Aristotle: The Desire to Understand*, Cambridge: Cambridge University Press, 1988, p. 27). I thank Howard Engelskirchen for the reference to Lear's work.

248 Aristotle (trans. Robin Waterfield), *Physics*, Oxford: Oxford University Press, 1996, p. 39, <II, 3, 194b23>.

249 Ibid., <II, 3, 194b26>.

250 Ibid., <II, 3, 194b29>.

251 Ibid., <II, 3, 194b32>.

252 Lear, *Aristotle: The Desire to Understand*, Chapter 2.

essence in *RTS* and *PON* does not involve the idea that entities (including societies) have potential identities that it is their inner purpose to realize. However, the notion of formal cause may be construed in non-teleological terms. Such a step moves us towards a more mechanistic conception of essence (such as that proposed by Locke), but can, I think, be combined with the retention of Aristotle's basic typology. Formal cause conceived non-teleologically refers still to a defining form or pattern; it is simply that the realization of form is no longer cast as a necessary, internally given goal.[253] The efficacy of social structures as critical realists conceive them is best understood in these terms. Social structures are pre-established, and in that sense objective, relationships that have determinate effects on individual agency. As such, they are analogous not to the wood out of which a house is built, but to the blueprint that determines whether it will be a bungalow or a mansion.

With respect to Varela's contention that even the ascription to structures of material causal efficacy is a reification of individual agency, I am inclined to respond that Varela has not offered much in the way of argumentation in defense of this view. At the level of metaphysics, Varela's claim amounts to a rejection of all but efficient (and perhaps final) cause. What is at stake, then, is the very idea of a variegated conception of causality. To put it differently, Varela would have us reclaim a neo-Aristotelian notion of efficient causality as the action of a powerful particular, yet maintain a post-Aristotelian ban on material and formal, if not final, cause. The weakness of Varela's case, however, is that it is circular: causality, he says, is efficient causality; therefore, he concludes, material and formal cause are reifications of efficient causality. The extension of the concept of causality is an issue that should be pursued further. However, there is a need for those who oppose the concepts of material and formal cause to offer a more developed defense of their position than Varela has given us.

At the level of philosophy of social science, meanwhile, the debate concerns the nature of agency. Apart from denying the very existence of so-called social structures (a substantive social theoretical claim,

---

253 Lear reminds us that for Aristotle the form of a thing presupposes something other than the thing itself as its source. As Lear puts it, for Aristotle "the order which exists at any level of matter is insufficient to generate the order required at the next level of organization" (Lear, *Aristotle: The Desire to Understand*, p. 39). This assumption represents a crucial metaphysical difference between Aristotelian essentialism and the more mechanistic essentialism, for a lack of a better way to put it, that Bhaskar, Ellis and even Harré and Madden propound.

which in a sense renders the rest of the analysis moot), here Varela
would have it that to ascribe efficacy to entities other than persons
inevitably leads one to endorse determinism with respect to individual agency. Any giving over of formal causal power to structures
represents a loss of freedom. In this regard, Varela has argued that it
is vital to appreciate that the structure/agency debate is a reformulation of the Kantian problematic of necessity versus freedom. On this
point I think that Varela is absolutely mistaken. In making it he
misses a key conceptual advantage of the very approach to causality
that he endorses.

Varela seems to think that the significance of realism about
causality in relation to social life is that it implies that agents, as the
only genuine sources of change, are in principle entirely unfettered by
any external (or internal, for that matter) constraints.[254] As we have
seen, any suggestion that this is not so is regarded as a conceptual
error of reification (though, curiously, Harré and Varela do not seem
overly concerned about the fact of real, material reification). What
Varela does not appreciate, however, is that realism about causality
of the sort proposed by Harré and Madden, as well as by Bhaskar,
allows us to set aside the Kantian problematic altogether. From a
transcendental realist perspective, causality is the exercise or display
of causal powers. Agency, from this perspective, is just the *intentional*
display of such powers. There is no dichotomy between the two. This
is a markedly different conception of agency than that of a noumenal
capacity that somehow escapes the rubric of law. Critical naturalists
such as Bhaskar regard structures and individuals alike to be bearers
of causal powers. Each has an effect on the other, although the
relationship is an asymmetrical one. Freedom, from such a perspective, has nothing to do with getting out from under structures *per se*,
let alone transcending causality. Instead, freedom has to do with the
establishment of structures that permit and sustain the full flourishing
of human capacities. From such a perspective, Varela's voluntarism
can be seen to undermine theoretical discussion about freedom in just
the same way as positivism does: both involve the denial of real
structural constraints on flourishing.

In sum, then, my response to Harré and Varela's "internal"
objections to critical realism is to stipulate that social structures
should be conceived as formal rather than efficient causes. As already
stated, I take the assertion that efficient causes are all there is to be a

---

254 Varela is also opposed to the concept of the unconscious, regarding it too as
a reification of the causal power of individuals. See op. cit., Varela, "The
Ethogenics of Agency and Structure: A Metaphysical Problem."

not-well-defended assumption. In my view, there is no obvious reason to collapse the concept of causality into that of efficient cause. As a philosophical matter, it seems to me intuitively clear that the extension of the former ought to exceed that of the latter. I regard the retheorization of causality in non-Humean terms as an opportunity to recover the richness, if not the underlying teleology, of the Aristotelian framework. As a sociological matter, meanwhile, I agree with Lewis, who argues that Harré and Varela's understanding of social structures as narrative strategies has less explanatory power than does the critical realist alternative.

Scientific essentialism

Brian Ellis calls the approach that he takes scientific essentialism. Scientific essentialism is a non-Humean metaphysics, at the heart of which is the thesis of dispositional realism.[255] Much as Bhaskar does – though Ellis employs a different vocabulary and develops the position in far greater detail – Ellis argues that substances are endowed with dispositional properties. To be the bearer of a dispositional property is to have the propensity to do specific things under specific conditions. Causal processes, says Ellis, consist precisely in the display of said dispositional properties. Causal laws connect antecedent and consequent events of given kinds by expressing what it is about the former (i.e., events of the kind of which the cause is) that brings into being the latter (namely, events of the kind of which the effect is). A proposed causal law may be erroneous. If it is true, however, it describes a metaphysical necessity. A causal law that is true, Ellis agrees with Bhaskar, is necessarily true – not because the assertion of its negation is a logical contradiction, but rather because it expresses the real necessity of a thing to display just those essential dispositional properties by virtue of which it is a member of one kind and not of another.

As does Bhaskar, Ellis believes that natural science is a matter of identifying the necessary relationships between the events or entities that we seek to explain and the underlying causal mechanisms that produce or constitute them, namely, the dispositional properties which are the real essences of natural kinds.[256] Unlike Bhaskar, however, Ellis maintains that such an account cannot be extended to

---

255 The following is a summary of Brian Ellis's position in op. cit., Ellis, *Scientific Essentialism*.
256 It should be noted that Ellis affirms the existence of natural kinds of processes and properties, as well natural kinds of substances.

the social sciences. Instead, he holds, "the traditional empiricist theory of the nature of scientific laws may thus be more or less right for the social sciences."[257] Ellis advances two different arguments in support of his position – a position that amounts, in context, to a firm anti-naturalism. The first argument is that even neo-classical economics, which Ellis takes to be the social science with the greatest claim to scientificity á la natural science, is not, in fact, fundamentally akin to natural science. The second argument is that scientific essentialism is inapplicable to the social sciences because social phenomena do not have essences. The first argument is the less forceful of the two, it seems to me; let me address it first, therefore, and then turn to what I see as the more significant challenge to critical naturalism.

(i) Ellis on the form of social science

Ellis points to three basic differences between neo-classical economics and natural sciences. The first difference is that economic laws do not refer to processes that are physically necessary.[258] The second difference is that neo-classical economics, according to Ellis, cannot support a Lakatosian distinction between the discipline's "hard core" and its "protective belt." In the social sciences, Ellis contends, any attempt to operate on the basis of such a distinction would be deemed ideological and thus non-scientific.[259] The third difference has to do with the character of models in economic theory. Neo-classical models, Ellis argues, are "quasi-analytic" mathematical constructs, rather than descriptions of essential processes.[260] They do not meet criteria for either theoretical soundness or empirical adequacy, as Ellis puts it.[261] Ellis's view is that economics – and social science more generally – is not well served either by (a) its actual a priori character or by (b) pretensions to the effect that it is – or should be – practiced according to the norms of natural science – i.e., in keeping with the model of scientific essentialism. Instead, he maintains, social scientists "must be empiricists in the old, and often maligned, sense of this term."[262] In short, he concludes, "Bacon's

257 Brian Ellis, *Scientific Essentialism*, p. 180.
258 It is not entirely clear whether by "economic law" Ellis is referring to knowledge claims of a specific type or to economic phenomena of a specific type. I shall continue to use the term "law" to refer to knowledge claims.
259 Ellis, *Scientific Essentialism*, pp. 183–186.
260 Ibid., p. 187 and p. 194.
261 Ibid., pp. 189–190.
262 Ibid., p. 197.

inductive methodology may not be wholly inappropriate for economics."[263]

Of the three qualitative differences that Ellis finds between natural science and neo-classical economics, only the first, it seems to me, is indisputable. But this is because it is trivial. The fact that social science concerns social relationships rather than physical ones tells us only that the social sciences do not have the same object domain as the natural sciences. But this is not news. Rather, it is the very basis for asking whether or not the two types of inquiry nonetheless ought to have the same form. It is only if we have already assumed that the only necessary connections that obtain are physical ones that the fact that social scientific laws are not physically necessary tells against the viability of scientific essentialism as a philosophy of social science.

The claim that social science is well described by empiricism because it is poorly described by Lakatos, meanwhile, invites a different sort of response. There are two points to be made here. Most important, while Ellis may look favorably upon Lakatos's views, there is no special connection between scientific essentialism, grounded upon dispositional realism, and Lakatos's account of scientific progress. Even if Ellis is right, and Lakatos's framework is totally inapplicable to social science, this does not imply that social science ought to be construed (and practiced) along classical empiricist lines. Beyond this, there are certainly those who would disagree with Ellis's assessment of Lakatos's relevance to social science.[264] Social science, many would say, does, in fact, develop via a progression of research programmes that are more fruitful than those that they replace. Moreover, the fundamental precepts of a successful social scientific research programme are no less likely to be abandoned lightly than are those of a successful research programme in the natural sciences. Indeed, the very fact that neo-classical economics seems invulnerable to empirical challenge – which Ellis cites as evidence of its proponents' "a priorism"[265] – is a clear example of a theoretical core being surrounded by a protective belt.[266] This is not to say that any research agenda with a protected theoretical core is therefore scientific, or to endorse Lakatos approach to the issue. I simply want to show that the use that Ellis makes of Lakatos is subject to criticism. Ellis might be expected to respond that even if some social scientists do both accept Lakatos's criterion

263 Ibid., p. 198.
264 Thanks to Doug Porpora for his thoughts on this issue.
265 Ellis, *Scientific Essentialism*, p. 197.
266 Thanks to Hugh Lacey for this point. Personal conversation, April 25, 2002.

of scientificity and maintain that social science fits the bill, his, Ellis's, point is that there is no *legitimate* basis – either ontological or epistemological – upon which the "core" of a social science research programme may be either delineated or protected. The ontological element of this claim is the proposition that social phenomena have no essential structures; the epistemological element is the proposition that adherence to favored models in the social sciences (neo-economics paradigmatically) is not well justified. I shall address the ontological point later. The epistemological point, meanwhile, is precisely the third component of Ellis's case that social science is entirely unlike natural science.

Here the argument is that scientific essentialism does not apply to the social sciences because neo-classical economic models do not meet what Ellis takes to be standard criteria within the natural sciences for theoretical soundness and empirical adequacy. Theoretical soundness, according to Ellis, requires that "the laws that are supposed to govern the objects in the model [be] theoretically derivable from . . . more fundamental laws that we are independently justified in accepting."[267] Empirical adequacy, meanwhile, requires a detailed causal account of the difference between reality and a proposed theoretical ideal. Neo-classical economics fails on both scores, Ellis tells us: economic "laws" cannot be reduced to more basic theories; actual economies don't behave the way neo-classical economists say they do.[268]

Now, I agree with the suggestion that neo-classical economics is neither sound nor adequate, but I am not led by this judgment to conclude that social reality is in fact well described by the implicit ontology of empiricism. The question is: does either of these points (if true, which I think that they are) give us reason to believe that causality itself is something different in the social world than it is in the natural world? I cannot see that they do. My response to the first point is the same as my response to the idea that dispositional realism is inapplicable to social science because social scientists seek to explain social rather than physical processes (and it is really the same idea that is being expressed here). The fact that social scientists theorize social rather than physical phenomena (and that explanations of the former cannot be reduced to explanations of the latter) only tells against the applicability of dispositional realism to the social world if one has already decided that physical properties alone can ground non-accidental connections. But such an assumption is

267 Ellis, *Scientific Essentialism*, p. 189.
268 Ibid., p. 190.

clearly question-begging. Meanwhile, the fact that neo-classical economics is a woefully inadequate explanatory framework implies only that it ought to be abandoned – and that it occupies the position of favor that it does for what must ultimately be non-epistemic reasons.

(ii) Ellis on social entities

Ellis's ontological argument is stronger than his epistemological argument. In critical realist parlance, the ontological argument concerns the nature of the intransitive, rather than the transitive, object of social scientific inquiry. The claim here is that scientific essentialism is inapplicable to social science because social phenomena lack essential structures on the basis of which to fall into natural kinds. It is this ontological thesis that Ellis's analysis of social science presupposes. I want to challenge Ellis's conclusions regarding social phenomena, but a few preliminary comments are in order. These, I hope, will provide the necessary context for the argument that I want to make.

To begin, Ellis's approach is not what one would expect it to be. Causality, for Ellis, is a matter of the display of dispositional properties. Affirmation of the existence of such properties is at the very heart of scientific essentialism. Accordingly, one would have expected the argument from Ellis against the extension of scientific essentialism to social phenomena to be based, as is that of Harré and Varela, on a claim that social phenomena are not party to dispositional displays – and this because they are not bearers of dispositional properties. But this is not the tack that Ellis takes. Instead, as I shall discuss in some detail, he pursues the idea that social phenomena have no fixed characteristics.

Second, while Ellis, like Bhaskar, focuses more on powers than on powerful particulars, Ellis conceptualizes the phenomenon of a causal power more narrowly than does Bhaskar. For Ellis, who more often uses the term "disposition," a causal power is the potential that a thing has to behave in a certain way (i.e., to display a dispositional property). For Bhaskar, meanwhile (as is implied in his explicit acknowledgement of material causality and in his implicit recognition of formal causality), almost any kind of determining function may legitimately be termed a power. So construed, the concept of a causal power includes but is more general than that of a disposition. When they are talking about physical processes, the difference in conceptual vocabulary between Ellis and Bhaskar is largely moot. Both hold that efficient causality, here paramount, is a matter of the exercise, as Bhaskar puts it, or display, as Ellis puts it, of powers that things have (or are) essentially.[269] These are powers in the more restrictive sense of the term – powers that things have to bring about changes in other things. When Bhaskar turns to social structures, however, he is saying something different. When he is talking about social structures, he is saying that causality, now implicitly construed as *formal* rather than efficient causality, is a matter of the "powers" (understood here in the much looser sense) that structures have to determine outcomes only inasmuch as they sustain and/or delimit possible courses of action. Ellis, meanwhile, is denying that structures have powers construed in the narrow sense – though he is not going about it by asserting that only persons can be agents, as do Harré and Varela, but rather by maintaining that structures have no essences.

It is crucial to distinguish between the sense in which efficient causality can be defined in terms of the display of a power and the sense in which formal (and final) causality can be defined in terms of the display of a power. With respect to social structures, the latter sense applies (if it does) to all social structures. The former sense, by contrast – as Rob Albritton points out – only applies to those social structures that are so reified as to exhibit, or at least seem to exhibit, agent-like behavior.[270] Albritton has argued that capital, for example, is such a power. Other, less reified structures, in Albritton's view, are only powers – if we want to even use the term – in a far less literal sense. It is extremely important to be able to make this distinction. To do so, however, requires that one not elide the difference between formal and efficient cause, as Bhaskar in my view tends to do. While I want to refrain from characterizing formal causality in dispositional terms, I do believe, as previously argued, that formal causes are efficacious. Moreover, I don't think that the refinement of categories that I have recommended has any negative implications for the viability of transcendental realism in relation to social phenomena. Causality, we may say, is a matter of powers that efficient causes have to effect change directly and/or a matter of the powers that formal (and final and material) causes have to effect change indirectly, by enabling, delimiting and/or motivating action.

Finally, while Ellis maintains that social phenomena lack essences, it is worth noting that he does not actually seem to be saying that they cannot be causes. I read him this way mainly because he shows no sign of subscribing to either ontological or methodological

---

269 For Ellis, things are what they are by virtue of what they can do. Bhaskar tends to talk about things being able to do what they can by virtue of what they are.
270 Personal conversation, June 2002.

individualism. He apparently has no objection to holism, to the idea that there are social objects that do not reduce to the aggregate behavior of individuals. Nor does he suggest that a proper social science would consist of the study of individuals. He is, admittedly, limited in his conception and analysis of social phenomena – focusing as he does on markets – but he is expressly concerned with how best to understand such phenomena scientifically.

As I've said, I want to argue against Ellis that realism about causality can be extended to the social world. My position is that social phenomena do have essential characteristics, and that it is by virtue of these that they regularly exercise the sort of powers borne by formal causes, and sometimes exercise powers that are similar to those borne by efficient causes. Given that Ellis bases his case against naturalism on the idea that social phenomena do not have such characteristics – and therefore cannot be said to fall into natural kinds – let me start off by trying to pinpoint exactly why it is that he makes such an assessment. The key idea seems to be that objects such as markets are "human constructs," as he puts it.[271] The question, then, is what is it about being a human construct that renders an object devoid of essential properties? Or, as Ellis would be more likely to put it, what is it about being a human construct that precludes social objects from falling into natural kinds? Sometimes it sounds as though Ellis is saying that social objects do not fall into natural kinds simply because members of natural kinds are natural objects, while social objects are social objects. But this doesn't tell us anything of importance. What we need to know is why one might think that social objects do not fall into natural kind analogues, i.e., into social kinds.

The argument against the existence of social kinds seems to be that because social phenomena are produced by human beings, they are mutable – radically so – in a way in which physical phenomena are not. There is also a suggestion that the objects of the social world do not fall into kinds because each particular is unique. "Market economies and market forces have no essential natures," Ellis writes.[272]

> Market forces are different, and behave differently, in different economies. They also behave differently in different sectors of the same economy, at different stages of its development, and at different times in the business cycle.[273]

271 Ellis, *Scientific Essentialism*, p. 179.
272 Ibid., p. 194.
273 Ibid.

A phenomenon that cannot be counted upon to retain its identity, Ellis seems to be saying, is patently ineligible to be the object of an essentialist research programme.

How might one defend critical naturalism against such an argument? There are two potential lines of response, it seems to me, one sociological and one philosophical. A sociological approach would center on an empirical analysis of what one takes to be legitimate examples of social kinds, e.g., value, the wage-relation, the commodity form, patriarchy.[274] A primarily philosophical response, meanwhile, involves taking a closer look at the logic of Ellis's position. This is the approach that I shall pursue. A number of possible objections to Ellis's case emerge from such an examination.

The first point to be made is that Ellis's conclusions rest upon an assessment of the relationship between objects having essences and objects undergoing change. The contention would seem to be that it is because social phenomena are subject to change that they are not candidates for having essential characteristics. Implicit in this claim is the idea that those objects that *do* have essences do not undergo change – or at least that they do not undergo changes in which they lose any of the properties that they hold essentially. But such a proposition is at odds with the behavior of the physical entities that Ellis himself accepts as paradigmatic instances of natural kinds. Water, for example, can lose the oxygen molecule that differentiates it from hydrogen, or can gain an extra hydrogen molecule, the addition of which transforms it into heavy water. An atom can be split apart. And so on.

If one joins with Ellis in accepting the existence of natural kinds, then what the example tells us is not that because water can undergo change it doesn't have an essence, but rather that when water loses its oxygen molecule it becomes something other than water, i.e., hydrogen. To put it differently, when something with an essence undergoes essential change, it doesn't *ipso facto* become something that never had an essence in the first place. It simply becomes something different from what it was before. As Danermark *et al.* put it:

> Here [in relation to the concept of natural necessity], "nature" in general terms refers to ... that which at a certain moment

274 Thanks to Howard Engelskirchen and Hans Ehrbar for their comments on value as a social kind; to Doug Porpora for his thoughts on the topic in general, and on patriarchy as a social kind in particular; and to the members of the Bhaskar listserv, for taking up this question in response to a query from me.

determines what a certain object is. The nature of the object may change, but then we will be dealing with a new object with other constitutive properties.[275]

Nor does the potential for change pose any special epistemological challenge. It is not necessary for an object to remain the same indefinitely in order for it to be studied scientifically, only that it do so for some determinate period of time. Indeed, the lower end of the range of such time frames is minute, as evidenced by the fleeting nature of the particles that constitute the object domain of subatomic physics. Whether or not social objects retain the properties by virtue of which they are things of one kind and not another long enough to be studied is an empirical question, the answer to which is yes. As a sociological matter, a critical realist will not be especially worried about this continuing to be the case. From the perspective of the TMSA, the ongoing existence of social structures is not in question on a moment-by-moment basis. Capitalist markets may be "human constructs," but they are not voluntaristically produced afresh each instant.

A second issue that emerges upon scrutiny of Ellis's position concerns variation between members of a given social kind. While he emphasizes their impermanence, Ellis also draws attention to the fact that the putative members of social kinds are not identical. In his words:

> The economy is a socially constructed system, heavily dependent on human conventions, and different economies have different mechanisms for achieving their objectives. Even market economies differ from each other in various ways, both structurally and in how they work (Hutton, 1996; Fukuyama, 1995). Consequently, we should not expect to find a unique and simple underlying reality for our economic theories to describe. [276]

Such difference amongst particulars is taken as further evidence that social phenomena do not share any essential characteristics. I am not convinced by the argument. Even in the case of infimic species, which admit of no further classification, there is no expectation that the members of a kind be identical in every single respect. Rather, they are expected to share only those properties that are essential to the

---

275 Danermark *et al.*, *Explaining Society: Critical Realism in the Social Sciences*, p. 44.
276 Brian Ellis, *Scientific Essentialism*, p. 187.

kind in question. There is no reason to think that things should be different with respect to social phenomena: variety amongst particulars does not weigh heavily against the existence of natural kind analogues. The fact that Canadian capitalism differs from Japanese capitalism does not imply that it is in the nature of the case that capitalism cannot be differentiated in kind from feudalism. Nor – to anticipate an objection that Ellis does not actually make – does the fact that there may be disagreement amongst social scientists regarding what the essential properties of a given kind are.

Ellis, of course – to return to the discussion of the character of social science for a moment – is opposed to the idea that there can be real definitions in social science. Insofar as capitalism, for example, can be characterized as having certain essential features, Ellis maintains that the terms of such an account can be only a priori, analytic definitions or empirical generalizations.[277] But I see no reason to accept this view. As in the natural sciences, real definitions in social science are propositions that, although they are developed through empirical analysis, capture real causal relationships in the world.[278] Even if Ellis is right, and I think he is, that neo-classical economics consists largely of empirically irrelevant model-building, it does not follow from this that economics as a social science should take the form of butterfly collecting.

The case that Ellis makes against social kinds is not persuasive. As "human constructs," social phenomena are, indeed, both varied and subject to change. Neither fact, however, supports the conclusion that they have no essential features – and thus cannot be the objects of real definitions. (Indeed, it is not even clear that social phenomena are unique in these regards.) However, Ellis's argument is problematic at an even deeper level. Ultimately, it seems to me, his position is unsatisfactory because it lands him in the untenable position of affirming that causality is one thing in the natural world and something entirely different (or perhaps non-existent) in the social world. For it is not just a matter of switching methodological hats – from that of scientific essentialism, according to which the purpose of inquiry is to establish real definitions, to that of classical empiricism, from the perspective of which science consists of generalizing from observation – when one turns one's attention to the social world.

---

277 Ibid., p. 193.

278 While they do not extend their account of causality to the social sciences as Bhaskar does, Harré and Madden offer a solid account of the process of generating real definitions in science. See Harré and Madden, *Causal Powers*, Chapter 1.

Certainly a scientific essentialist may be a pluralist about method. He or she may maintain, for example, that social entities have real essences, but there are times when nothing beats old-fashioned observation for yielding insight into what they are. But this is not what Ellis is saying. Rather, in offering a domain-specific endorsement of empiricism, which is ontologically rather than epistemologically grounded, Ellis is telling us that causality as he defines it – namely, a relationship of necessity that holds between event-kinds, in virtue of the dispositional properties that they display – does not apply to social phenomena.

This, it seems to me, is not a viable position. It would be different if Ellis were to reject the existence of social objects altogether, in favor of atomism. Then, at least, we could say that there are no relations of cause and effect between social phenomena because objects such as "markets" do not really exist. But Ellis acknowledges the existence of social entities, even if he doesn't fully register their relational character. He acknowledges the existence of social entities, but says that they do not enter into relationships of cause and effect, as he has defined that relationship. A determined defender of Ellis might say "Well, why can't we be pluralists about causal necessity? Maybe causality *is* one thing in the natural world and one thing in the social world." This strikes me as implausible, but in any case the response doesn't get off the ground in this instance because the recommended alternative account (i.e., that which is implicit in classical empiricism) is one in which natural necessity is thought not to exist. The conclusion to which I believe we must come is this: if, as Ellis argues, causality is a matter of what an entity can do, then this must be so for social entities (and persons) as well as for physical entities. The relationship of cause and effect is not domain-specific to the natural world. If scientific essentialists are right that causality is a matter of the real powers that things have to effect change, then it is so uniformly.

Let me take a quick moment to forestall a potential misunderstanding. In claiming that causality is the same "thing" universally, I am not affirming reductionism in any form. To say that the definition of causality is a constant is not to say that all events have the same, or even the same kinds of, causes. Nor does the idea that social phenomena have essential properties imply that such properties are physical ones. Bhaskar himself (with whom I would agree here) is quite clear in *PON* that he is opposed to materialist reductionism, both as an ontological stance and as an epistemological project. In contrast to reductionism, Bhaskar puts forward what he calls "synchronic emergent powers materialism" (SEPM). SEPM is the view that social (and mental) phenomena supervene upon the material conditions of

their existence; they emerge from – and are thus existentially contingent upon – but do not reduce to, their material components.
Emergent entities are non-reducible wholes that are qualitatively
distinct from the sum of their material parts. They do not reduce to
their components ontologically because they display – or have the
potential to display – properties that are not borne by their constituent
elements. They do not reduce epistemologically because the explanations in which they figure must refer to the properties that they, but
not their components, bear and/or bear essentially. Thus, in saying
that the capitalist wage-relation, for example, has a real essence
(namely, the transfer of surplus value), one is not saying that it can be
reduced to something that is non-social.

Causal powers and individuals

Bhaskar begins his discussion of individual agency by asking "What
properties [do] people possess that might make them objects of
knowledge for us?"[279] Here, as in the analysis of social structures,
what is really being asked is "What would intentional behavior have
to be like, in order for the model of science associated with
transcendental realism to be applicable to the study of it – and does it
meet said criteria?" As I understand him, Bhaskar's answer is that in
order for transcendental realism to hold *vis-à-vis* intentional behavior,
it would have to be the case that actions are caused by generative
mechanisms. Bhaskar holds that actions are undertaken as a result of
the mental states of actors. Much of the argument of Chapter 3 of
PON therefore centers on the proposition that it is legitimate to think
of mental states as generative mechanisms – or, to put it differently, to
think of reasons as causes.

The question of whether or not realism about causality can be
extended to individual agency does not seem to me to be a difficult
one to settle. That human beings are bearers of dispositional powers I
regard as beyond dispute. I am prepared to say that we bear such
powers essentially, albeit not uniquely. This is all that is required, it
seems to me, in order to affirm realism about causality in the
psychological domain. Bhaskar develops the case further, however. As
I have indicated, he maintains not just that people are bearers of
causal powers, but that, in the case of action, the exercise of such
powers is itself brought about and/or constrained by reasons. This
gets him to the idea that it is reasons (rather than actors) that are the
psychological analogue of generative mechanisms in nature.

279 Bhaskar, *PON*, p. 80.

I have no objection to the claim that reasons are causally efficacious – and since, in my view, realism about causality does not depend on the validity of such a proposition, I am not going to take the time to rehearse Bhaskar's argument on its behalf. I do, however, want to intervene in the discussion at the point at which it has been established that reasons are causally relevant. Specifically, I want to suggest that Bhaskar makes two mistakes in how he theorizes intentional processes. The first mistake is that he casts reasons in the role of efficient causes. The second is that he conceives of action as a sub-type of physical event, rather than as the material enactment of purpose. It is important to see that I have not simply described the same mistake in two different ways. In the first case, we are given an incorrect – or at least imprecise and potentially misleading – answer to the question "In what sense are reasons causally efficacious?" In the second case, we are given an incorrect answer to the question "What are actions?"

My view is that reasons are final causes, not efficient causes. Actions, meanwhile, although motivated by reasons, cannot be resolved conceptually into a set of physical behaviors brought about by an antecedent emotional/mental state. Instead they must be conceived as being inherently meaningful. They are "singular structural unit[s]" of intentionality, to use Varela and Harré's phrase.[280] I think that it is important to distinguish between these two points, as there is ultimately no necessary connection between them. The fact that reasons are not efficient causes (that, rather, they are the purposes for which actions are undertaken), does not tell us what actions are. Conversely, the fact that actions are something other than behavior does not tell us what sort of efficacy we may appropriately ascribe to reasons. I don't believe that this distinction has been made clearly enough by those within the hermeneutic tradition who have argued for the place of final cause in the explanation of action.

I am not going to spend a great deal of time arguing the first point. Bhaskar maintains that to say that reasons cannot be efficient causes is to commit what he calls "the 'essentialist fallacy' of holding that the only real causes are ultimate ones."[281] Presumably, if we are to avoid committing the essentialist fallacy, we must affirm that "real" causes are efficient causes, and that this category includes reasons. In keeping with this line of reasoning, Bhaskar specifies that it is reasons that are the psychological analogues of causal mechanisms in

280 Varela and Harré, "Conflicting Varieties of Realism: Causal Powers and the Problems of Social Structure," p. 322.
281 Bhaskar, *PON*, p. 84.

nature.[282] "Teleological explanations," he contends, "are most naturally construed as a species of ordinary causal explanation, where the
cause is, in the case of reasons, some antecedent state of mind."[283] In
this instance I believe that Bhaskar has – as Harré and Varela charge
he has done with respect to social structures – simply ascribed agent-
like properties to a kind of thing, namely, mental states, that is not, in
fact, agent-like. Reasons, I think we have to say, are final causes.
They are why actions are undertaken. They are not, however, the
powerful particulars that enact them. I don't believe that such a
stipulation poses any problem for critical realism. As in the case of
social structures, we do not need to say that reasons are efficient
causes in order to say that they have determining effects. It is perhaps
worth noting that it is not clear whether Bhaskar means to say that it
is reasons themselves, or the holding of reasons, that are causes.[284] I
think that he is inconsistent on this point, at least at the level of
rhetoric. On the one hand, he states "[t]hus, the possession of a
reason, conceived as a more or less long-standing disposition or orientation to act in a certain way, may itself be a cause."[285] On the other
hand, he repeatedly and emphatically expresses his position as being
the view that "reasons" are causes. In the end, I am not sure that it
matters. The holding of a reason does not seem to me to be any more
of a powerful particular than are reasons themselves.

The second point, having to do with the concept of action, is more
complicated. Here my contention is that Bhaskar does not distinguish
adequately and consistently between action and behavior. I shall
make the case in part via the work of Charles Taylor. It is important
to appreciate, however, that Taylor himself tends to run together the
two different issues that I have identified as being problematic in
Bhaskar's treatment of agency, namely, that of the causal properties
of reasons and that of the depiction of action. Taylor's implicit
presumption is that the fact that reasons are final causes and the fact
that actions are irreducibly meaningful are one and the same point. I
am suggesting that this is not so – that it is possible to be differently
(and independently) mistaken about what reasons can and cannot do,
on the one hand, and about what actions are and are not, on the
other.

282 Ibid.
283 Ibid.
284 Thanks to Hugh Lacey for this point. Personal conversation, June 17, 2002.
     Lacey defends Bhaskar against the charge of reifying reasons, maintaining that for
     Bhaskar it is the holding of a reason by an agent that is efficacious, not the reason
     itself.
285 Bhaskar, *PON*, p. 85.

In an article entitled "Hegel's Philosophy of Mind," Taylor identifies two different ways of conceptualizing action.[286] One approach – which Taylor dubs the "causal view" – is to think of actions as being events like any others. The only thing that distinguishes actions from other events, from this perspective, is that they happen to have psychological causes. As Taylor puts it, "[a]ctions are events which are peculiar in that they are brought about by desires, or intentions, or combinations of desires and beliefs."[287] Taylor associates this approach with Cartesian dualism, in that actions are viewed as physical events with non-material causes. The alternative approach, which Taylor calls the "qualitative view," is to think of actions as differing ontologically from other events. From this perspective, what is unique about actions is not simply that, unlike other events, they are motivated by reasons, but that actions and their "causes" cannot be disaggregated. Actions, from this perspective, just *are* the expressions of purposes; they cannot be characterized first in non-purposive terms, and only then, retroactively as it were, connected to a mental or emotional state.

Taylor, predictably, advances the latter, "qualitative" approach. Bhaskar, meanwhile, must be seen in *PON* to be a espousing the "causal" view. "[A]ctions," he writes, "[are] regarded (paradigmatically) as the class of bodily movements with reasons as their causes."[288] For Taylor, as for proponents of hermeneutic social science generally, actions are irreducibly meaningful. As a result, they cannot be correctly identified in non-purposive terms. Bhaskar, by contrast, holds that while actions *may* be characterized in such terms, they "can also normally be redescribed independently of their reasons."[289] Although it has immediate epistemological implications, the underlying dispute is ontological: Bhaskar sees actions as a subclass of bodily movements; Taylor sees actions as signs. If Taylor is right, then Bhaskar's account of what it is to explain intentional behavior is flawed from the outset.

Now I want to be very careful here. There are in fact two different theses in circulation. The first is that actions are inherently meaningful. The second is that there is no way to disaggregate actions from their causes. My view is that Taylor is right to think that

---

286 Charles Taylor, *Human Agency and Language: Philosophical Papers 1*, Cambridge: Cambridge University Press, 1985, Chapter 3. My discussion of Taylor's argument in Chapter 3 is informed by the content of Chapters 1 and 4.
287 Ibid., p. 78.
288 Bhaskar, *PON*, p. 88.
289 Ibid.

actions are inherently meaningful, but wrong to imply, as I think that he does, that we cannot distinguish between the meaning that an action expresses and that which caused the agent to act. The meaning of an action does not necessarily tell us why an actor undertook to express such a meaning. Take Taylor's own example of voting: marking off a box on a piece of paper, he says, is not the same thing as casting a vote. The latter is what it is in part because of the inter-subjectively held meanings that it has. However, I can be identified as having voted without it being apparent what my reasons were for doing so. A satisfactory account of my action would have to explain not just *what* I was doing, but *why* I was doing it. I think that Bhaskar can be read as trying to make just this point. Unfortunately, in the course of arguing that we can distinguish between actions and their causes, he winds up saying that we can distinguish between actions and their meanings.

Let me elaborate. In an early article entitled "Emotion, Behavior and Belief,"[290] Alasdair MacIntyre describes a scenario in which a man crosses the street in order to avoid someone with whom he has had a disagreement. This same man, MacIntyre says, could just as well have taken other steps to signal his displeasure. For example, he could have (in a fairly outlandish move) purchased the entire supply of a rare fruit that the person who angered him enjoys. Equally plausible, he could have taken steps to prevent the person from receiving a desired invitation to a party. "Crossing a road, buying up fruit, stealing mail: these actions have nothing in common with each other and yet they can all express resentment," MacIntyre writes.[291] Conversely, any one of these acts could, qua bodily movements, easily be undertaken for reasons totally unrelated to such expression. The point that MacIntyre makes is that it is not possible to tell, on the basis of observed behavior, whether crossing the street is an instance of resentment or simply of being preoccupied. As in Taylor's example of voting, in order to be able to identify a sequence of bodily movements as an action of one sort or another, we must know its purpose. MacIntyre's claim is an epistemological one, but it is sound in virtue of the underlying ontological one: behavior and action are not the same thing. Unlike behavior, action is meaningful. If we don't know what an action is intended to express, we don't know what it is.

MacIntyre's criticism of behaviorism applies to Bhaskar's depiction of actions. Bhaskar of course rejects behaviorism. The mistake,

290 Alasdair MacIntyre, *Against the Self-images of the Age: Essays on Ideology and Philosophy*, Notre Dame, IN: University of Notre Dame Press, 1978, Chapter 20.
291 Ibid., p. 231.

however, is in nonetheless retaining the idea that actions are such that they can be characterized in non-purposive terms. It is perfectly legitimate to hold that the explanation of action must involve the identification of the beliefs and/or desires that led to a specified act. A specified act, however, is already something other than a sequence of bodily movements. As I have said, I think that Bhaskar can be read as simply trying to say that the question of *why* an action was undertaken is not given by the answer to the question of *what* the action expresses, or signifies. Indeed, there are enough places in *PON* where he seems to acknowledge the intrinsic meaningfulness of the social world that one is tempted to disregard his claim that actions can be redescribed as behavior. However, he does make it, along with the claim that action is best defined as behavior that is caused (i.e., efficiently caused) by reasons. It is therefore incumbent upon defenders of critical realism to register the problems that are associated with such an approach.

In this spirit, let me return to Taylor for a moment. In articles entitled "The Concept of a Person" and "What Is Human Agency?" Taylor argues that the Cartesian approach to agency is connected to an impoverished view of human nature.[292] I believe that this is a line of analysis worth pursuing, if only to underscore the importance of conceptualizing action in non-Cartesian terms. In "The Concept of a Person," Taylor once again establishes a juxtaposition between the Cartesian approach to agency and a hermeneutic alternative. He begins by posing two questions for the purposes of orientation. The first is "In virtue of what is an entity rightly thought to be an agent?" The second is "What is the difference between human beings and other kinds of agent?" From the Cartesian perspective, the answer to both questions is the same: agenthood is ascribed on the basis of an entity's capacity for representation, and it is only human beings who have such a capacity. From the hermeneutic perspective, by contrast, what makes an entity an agent is that it can generate its own ends. What distinguishes human beings from other agents – for we are not the only creatures who can generate our own ends – is not our capacity to employ signs (though it may be that this ability is unique to us), but rather the fact that we are capable of generating, and responding to, ends that are normative. Taylor refers to these as "peculiarly human concerns," openness to which, as he puts it, constitutes consciousness in a sense which is not conveyed by the concept of abstract representation.[293]

---

292 Taylor, *Human Agency and Language: Philosophical Papers 1*, Chapters 1 and 4.
293 Ibid., pp. 104–105.

Both models allow that human beings are capable of self-con-sciousness and self-direction.[294] Proponents of the Cartesian approach, however, associate these traits with the ability to plan – a talent that is taken to be greatly enhanced by our capacity for abstract representation. Proponents of the hermeneutic approach, meanwhile, associate such traits with the ability to engage in what Taylor calls "strong," as opposed to "weak" evaluation.[295] Strong evaluation is reasoning about "the qualitative *worth* of different desires."[296] Weak evaluation, by contrast, is simply a ranking of alternative desires by preference. Taylor's thesis is that strong evaluation is "deeper" than weak evaluation. It requires "articulacy" – Taylor's term – not just about what we do want, but about what we believe that we *ought* to want. "To characterize one desire or inclination as worthier, or nobler, or more integrated, etc. than others," Taylor writes,

> is to speak of it in terms of the kind of quality of life which it expresses and sustains. . . . Whereas for the simple weigher what is at stake is the desirability of different consummations, those defined by his *de facto* desires, for the strong evaluator reflection also examines the different possible modes of being of the agent.[297]

The point I want to make is that the account of agency that we find in *PON* levels distinctions such as that between strong and weak evaluation. Bhaskar presents all ends as being equally objects of desire. Moral ends are simply one type of good that a person might choose to pursue. I might desire to live a life marked by kindness, creativity and intellectual virtue. I might also like to have lasagna for supper. As they relate to action, there are no philosophically significant differences between these two desires. "One does what one wants to (or intends) unless prevented," Bhaskar writes. "This is a necessary truth. And no further explanation of action as such is required."[298] Now I do not want to be misunderstood here. I am not suggesting that Bhaskar intends to endorse either the utilitarian principle that the satisfaction of desire is the only good or the emotivist proposition that moral claims can be translated into statements of preference.[299] Nonetheless, there is at least an impetus

---

294 Ibid., p. 103.
295 Ibid., p. 16.
296 Ibid.
297 Ibid., p. 25.
298 Bhaskar, *PON*, p. 96.
299 Taylor discusses the link between utilitarianism and the conflation of strong and weak evaluation in op. cit., "What Is Human Agency?"

towards this kind of moral theory in the depiction of action in *PON*. At a minimum, this is further reason to revise the approach taken there.

I have concentrated in this section on the concept of action. Flagged by the conflation of action and behavior, however, is a more general concern. There is, I think, simply an under-appreciation in Bhaskar's early work of what is unique to the theorizing of concept-dependent objects. I don't want to be thought unfair about this. Bhaskar does state as a basic rule that

> inasmuch as the ontological claim is made that the social world is already constituted as meaningful, prior to the application of scientific theory to it, then a clear difference between it and the natural world must be accepted.[300]

And yet there is something missing. Addressing the problem of how to determine the meaning of a stated belief, Bhaskar tells us that we can achieve a "general resolution" of the problem as soon as we realize that the task "is only a special case of the para-hermeneutic problem of the correct identification of phenomena in science."[301] In both situations, he says, "the general problem of the underdetermin-ation of theory by experience is resolved by choosing the *theory which is phenomenally* (descriptively) *most adequate.*"[302] I am sympathetic to this argument at a certain level of generality. After all, a real definition is simply a theory about what something is. In the end, what is there to do but to endorse the theory that seems to offer the greatest amount of insight into the nature of the phenomena in question? But even if this is right, it is not enough. The problem is that Bhaskar's resolution bypasses any real discussion of the difficulty itself, which is that interpretations of text-analogues, to use Taylor's terminology, are not the same thing as real definitions of non-text analogues, or hypotheses concerning the causal relationships between them.[303] It is unfortunate that Bhaskar ultimately glosses over the

---

300 Bhaskar, *PON*, p. 85.
301 Ibid., p. 111.
302 Ibid.
303 While I do not have time to explore the connection here, I believe that the inattention to interpretation in critical naturalism is related not just to the idea that action can be redescribed in non-intentional terms, but also to the philo-sophy of language that Bhaskar develops in op. cit., *Plato, Etc.* Unsurprisingly, Bhaskar's approach is, in Taylor's terms again, designative rather than expressive. The emphasis is on words referring to objects, rather than on the ways in which meaning may constitute certain kinds of objects.

issue of interpretation in the way that he does. It is a detriment not just because having done so weakens critical naturalism, but also because the omission draws attention away from the fact that the TMSA allows for a non-subjectivist ontology regarding just those meaning-saturated phenomena the identities of which must be grasped hermeneutically.

Conclusion

Let me try to pull together the various threads of this discussion. The basic thesis that I have advanced in this chapter is that realism about causality can indeed be extended to the social world. I take this to be the fundamental metaphysical issue at stake in the present discussion. Having endorsed this basic component of critical naturalism, however, I have suggested that it is necessary to acknowledge the difference between the powers associated with efficient causes, on the one hand, and those associated with formal and final causes, on the other. Such a move allows for the typology of entities within the TMSA (in which the categories are structures and individuals) and the typology of generative mechanism analogues within critical naturalism (in which the categories are structures and reasons) to be integrated into a more finely articulated overall framework. Within such an amended framework, structures are seen to be bearers of formal causality (and only rarely, if ever, of efficient or efficient-like causality), which means that they have the power to enable and/or delimit possible courses of action. Individuals, meanwhile, are seen to be bearers of efficient causality, which means that they have the power to effect changes in other objects directly, whether intentionally or unintentionally. Reasons, finally, are understood to be final causes. Like formal causes such as structures, they have the power to motivate and/or undermine potential courses of action, but are not themselves agents.

Apart from suggesting a refinement of the notion of a causal power – in keeping with the richness of Aristotle's conception of causality – I have also taken issue with Bhaskar's account of action. Specifically, I have argued that Bhaskar is wrong to characterize action as a sub-type of behavior. Here I have tried to retain both what is right about the hermeneutic thesis that action is inherently meaningful, and what is right about Bhaskar's claim that actions are caused by reasons. Critical naturalism, it seems to me, in principle allows for satisfactory answers to two different questions. In response to the question "What is action?" we can say that action is best understood as the enactment of meaning, not behavior-with-a-certain-kind-of-cause. To the question "What causes action?" we can say that it is reasons (or the holding of reasons) that are the (final) causes of action.

Finally, I suggested that critical naturalism is not well served by Bhaskar's cursory treatment of the philosophical issues related to interpretation. Here especially, I think that there is more that remains to be learned from proponents of the hermeneutic approach. At the same time, I do believe that it is not enough to understand *what* is happening in a given context; we also need to know *why* it is happening. Theorists such as Taylor have interesting things to say about interpretation, but less to say about the construction of causal accounts. In Taylor's case, this can be seen in his vision of social science: social science is construed as being a kind of collective self-consciousness raising, in which we test out alternate "self-definitions," as he puts it, by seeing what kinds of practices they generate.[304] Taylor does not dispense with causal concerns altogether. In fact, he notes that "where and to the extent that social action has been informed by self-understanding, this will have to figure in any valid explanatory account."[305] Nonetheless, there is, on the whole, far more of an emphasis on identification than on explanation.

As I have said, Bhaskar presents himself as having achieved a synthesis of hermeneutic and causal approaches to social science. I think that critical naturalism as it is formulated in *PON* is not yet such a synthesis, although it has the potential to afford one. I argued earlier that critical naturalism in principle allows both for a definition of action as inherently meaningful and for the explanation of action in causal terms. Similarly, I believe that it can accommodate both a full appreciation of the necessarily interpretive nature of social science and the goal of identifying the causes of social phenomena.

Critical naturalism has the meta-theoretical potential that it does for two reasons. First, it is an approach in which causality and regularity have been decoupled. As a result, it is not subject to criticisms of causal approaches that are based on the particularity of social events. MacIntyre, for example, offers such a critique in another classic article entitled "Is a Science of Comparative Politics Possible?" and again in *After Virtue*.[306] Once one discards the Humean problematic, however, the fact that social phenomena do

304 Charles Taylor, "Social Theory as Practice," in *Philosophy and the Human Sciences: Philosophical Papers* 2, Cambridge: Cambridge University Press, 1985.
305 Ibid., p. 113.
306 Alasdair MacIntyre, *Against the Self-images of the Age: Essays on Ideology and Philosophy*, Notre Dame, IN: University of Notre Dame Press, 1978, Chapter 22 and op. cit., *After Virtue*.

not exhibit perfectly regular behavior has little bearing on whether or not such events are caused. Second, critical naturalism is compatible – or at least can be made compatible – with Aristotle's breaking down of the concept of causality into efficient, formal, final and material causality. At least in part, the divide between hermeneutic and naturalist approaches to social science is the result of a tacit acceptance amongst the proponents of each camp that "causality" refers to efficient causality. While I have suggested that Bhaskar himself has a tendency to try to fit formal and final causes (which he at least regards as legitimately causal) into the category of efficient causality, I believe that critical naturalism is in principle consistent with a non-teleological adaptation of the Aristotelian schema. If one adopts such a framework, the fact that social phenomena are meaning-laden has no significant bearing on whether or not they are caused. Of course, this is simply a sketch of what might be of value in critical naturalism, beyond its metaphysical core; I make no claim to have presented anything beyond a general comment on the matter. It is only the core that I have sought to defend in the present discussion.

6 Conclusion

Critical realism and the post-positivist quagmire

Having done my best in the foregoing chapters both to defend and to test the limits of critical realism, I want to conclude by returning to my basic contention regarding its significance. Critical realism, I proposed, can be of help in moving us beyond the post-positivist intellectual quagmire in which we find ourselves. The obvious first question to be asked in relation to such a claim is: to what extent does critical realism enable us to respond to the challenges of relativism and the anti-realism upon which relativism depends? Beyond this, what insights may be gained from adopting a critical realist stance that might allow us to make further headway?

(i)

Let me begin by considering critical realism as a rejoinder to relativism. From one angle, relativism can be seen as having to do with the concept of truth. Parsed in this way, relativism is tantamount to the idea that what it means for a proposition to be true is that it is affirmed by a given individual or group of individuals. From another angle, relativism can be conceived as a global epistemic assessment to the effect that all knowledge claims are equally well justified. Relativism construed as a theory of truth does not necessarily imply relativism construed as a theory of knowledge, if I may put it in such non-standard terms, as it is possible in the former scenario to distinguish epistemically between those views that a given audience accepts, and would therefore count as true, and those that they reject, and would therefore count as false. Nor, strictly speaking, does the second formulation imply the first. In principle, for example, one could hold to a correspondence theory of truth and yet – assuming a perfectly malleable referent (or, in epistemic rather than ontological terms, the thesis of radical under-determination)[307] – maintain that all claims capture to an equal degree the reality of that to which they refer.

In my view, an adequate response to relativism requires both a sound, non-epistemic theory of truth and a rejection of the idea that all knowledge claims are equally well founded. I believe that critical realism gives us the latter – albeit only indirectly – but not the former. While his efforts to theorize the concept of truth fall short, Bhaskar's naturalism about causality (and attendant commitment to the existence of natural kinds and real essences) provides a satisfactory ontological counter to relativism about knowledge. Moreover, I would add that critical realism points us in the right direction with respect to the concept of truth, even if Bhaskar himself veers off on a less promising course.

It is important to be clear about the nature of the check on relativism that Bhaskar's ontology provides. The fact that causal processes are based on the exercise of real powers that objects bear or are essentially tells us that the world is not all possible ways. It has definite characteristics, beyond extension. Such characteristics render those causal laws that do exist metaphysically necessary – our ability to imagine worlds in which there are unicorns whose cells freeze when heated notwithstanding. That this is so has epistemological implications. Specifically, it implies that it cannot be the case that all claims about the world are equally valid. That the world is all possible ways is not, however, a criterion of justific-ation: it cannot help us at all in deciding which ways the world actually (or potentially) is. Epistemically, then, naturalism about causality functions as a limiting principle only. It allows us to rule out the suggestion that all claims about the world are in a meaningful sense equally true, but nothing more. I do not want to say "merely" here, as the limit imposed is absolutely crucial. But it is important to keep in mind that the check that it provides is a formal one.

I have been quite clear in my opposition to Bhaskar's theory of truth, and I have acknowledged that he does not offer an account of justification. Nonetheless, critical realism does contain several key epistemic principles. The first is the check on relativism just described. Another is the thesis that knowledge is always only provisional. A third is the belief that it is possible to evaluate competing theories on

307 Larry Laudan, "'The Sins of the Fathers . . . ': Positivist Origins of Postpositivist Relativisms," in *Beyond Positivism and Relativism: Theory, Method and Evidence*, Boulder, CO: Westview Press, 1996, pp. 19–21. See also "Demystifying Underdetermination," in the same volume.

cognitive grounds. As should be evident, these three principles correspond to the three points in relation to which I explicated critical
realism in Chapter 1 – with the caveat that ontological realism has
here been given epistemological expression. I think that if one holds
to all three of these principles, one will be inclined to take the kind of
approach to the concept of truth, and to the relationships between
truth, justification, knowledge claims and belief, that I began to
sketch out in Chapter 4. As I suggested there, I believe that the
concept of truth, construed in minimalist correspondence terms, must
be understood to be no more, or less, than a transcendental condition
of possibility of inquiry itself. I read Davidson (2000) as saying
something similar in "Truth Rehabilitated." To quote a lengthy
passage:

> Sentences are understood on condition that one has the concept
> of objective truth. This goes also for the various propositional
> attitudes sentences are used to express. It is possible to have a
> belief only if one knows that beliefs may be true or false. I can
> believe it is now raining, but this is because I know that whether
> or not it is raining does not depend on whether I believe it, or
> everyone believes it, or it is useful to believe it . . . Truth enters
> into the other attitudes in other ways. We desire that a certain
> state of affairs be true, we fear, hope or doubt that things are one
> way or another. We intend by our actions to make it true that we
> have a good sleep. We are proud or depressed that it is the case
> that we have won the second prize. Since all these, and many
> more attitudes have a propositional content – the sort of content
> that can be expressed by a sentence – to have any of these
> attitudes is necessarily to know what it would be for the corres-
> ponding sentence to be true. Without a grasp of the concept of
> truth, not only language, but thought itself, is impossible.[308]

Adorno expresses what I take to be the same basic insight in the
following characteristically pithy comment: "the appearance of
identity is inherent in thought itself, in its pure form. To think is to
identify."[309]

As noted in Chapter 4, the approach that I am advancing has
the effect of driving a wedge between the concepts of truth and
justification, while at the same time blurring the boundary between

308 Donald Davidson, "Truth Rehabilitated," in Robert B. Brandom (ed.), *Rorty and His Critics*, Malden, MA: Blackwell Publishers, 2000], p. 72.
309 Adorno, *Negative Dialectics*, p. 5.

knowledge claims and belief (thereby casting serious doubt on the value of retaining the concept of "knowledge" defined as a body of justified, true beliefs).[310] This may bring us closer to Rorty's position, in particular, than some fellow critics of post-positivism would like. After all, Rorty too would have us break the bond between truth and justification, and be done with the traditional line of demarcation between knowledge claims and justified beliefs. The potential concern would seem to be that if we accept that the concept of truth has no direct bearing on justification, we wind up endorsing relativism about knowledge claims. I don't think that this is so. I don't see any necessary connection between a lack of epistemic certainty and the idea that all beliefs are equally valid. On the contrary, I am suggesting that we embrace a set of epistemic principles in which fallibilism is explicitly combined with the view that it *cannot* be the case that all beliefs about the world are equally valid.

I will concede that a fair amount of epistemic weight does fall, in the approach that I am defending, on the actual practice of deliberation. But I don't believe that this is cause for alarm. With respect to justification, I think that we simply have to accept that we cannot have absolute certainty. We can know *what* it is for a proposition to be true – and that, as best as we can tell, the world is such that it cannot be that *all* propositions are true. Beyond this, we are on our own, as it were, to offer reasons why we judge a given theory to be superior to another. Such a depiction of "rationality at the level of judgment," to use Bhaskar's terminology, is at odds with the foundational approach to epistemology that has been dominant since Descartes, and which runs through the history of Western philosophy, but it amounts neither to a disavowal of the concept of truth nor to the claim that all beliefs are equally valid.

Considered in relation to anti-realism, meanwhile, I believe that critical realism affords a compelling response to the idea that reality has no intrinsic structure. As observed in Chapter 1, critical realism is especially interesting in this regard because it shifts the focus away from the ontological status of disputed entities and onto the nature of causality. I shall pursue the broader implications of this shift in a moment. Here let me just say that the approach to causality that Bhaskar takes forces the question of whether or not the "something" external (which many thinkers don't want to deny the existence of) can plausibly be thought to be entirely indeterminate. In my view, Bhaskar (and Harré and Madden and Ellis) has shown that such an

---

310 This formulation is the result of discussion with Esteve Morera and Henry Laycock; the view expressed is mine alone.

ontology cannot, in fact, sustain a viable account of scientific explanation (or, as only Bhaskar argues, of social life).

Without the ontological thesis that reality has no intrinsic structure, however, we are left with a purely epistemic claim regarding the under-determination of theory by data (or, in Bhaskar's terminology, with nothing other than an acknowledgement of the ontic fallacy). In my opinion, Larry Laudan has done a good job of showing that neither Quine nor Kuhn ever in fact establishes the most extreme version of the thesis of under-determination, namely, that any body of evidence is equally compatible with an infinite number of explanations.[311] Less extreme versions, meanwhile – e.g., that there are likely to be rival theories that account equally well for a given body of evidence – deliver far less punch than is claimed by proponents of post-positivist perspectivism. The fact that explanations cannot be uniquely deductively inferred from a neutral observation language is old news. It hardly signals the "end of innocence," as Jane Flax would have it.

(ii)

Beyond helping us to counter the challenges of relativism and anti-realism, critical realism is of value because it illuminates the ontological roots of post-positivism. The result is to further develop an already-trenchant line of analysis undertaken within the philosophy of science by, for instance, Laudan. Laudan has shown that the post-positivist position has a positivist *epistemological* core.[312] It is not just that post-positivist thinkers tacitly endorse the traditional conception of knowledge as being value-free and absolutely certain – and so, finding that no theories actually meet these criteria, are forced to conclude that all that we thought to be *episteme* is in fact *doxa*, as Calvin Schrag has put it.[313] More technically, Laudan argues, Kuhn, for instance, accepts that theory comparison is best understood as being a "translation exercise" (thereby establishing a basis for the indeterminacy of translation thesis to be taken to imply the incommensurability of inter-paradigmatic theories), that the rationality of science hinges on the possibility of such operations and that all other norms of scientific

311 Laudan, *Beyond Positivism and Relativism: Theory, Method, and Evidence*, Chapters 1 and 2.
312 Ibid.
313 Calvin O. Schrag, *The Resources of Rationality: A Response to the Postmodern Challenge*, Bloomington: Indiana University Press, 1992, pp. 167–168.

inquiry, being neither "facts" nor analytic truths, are conventions that cannot be defended on cognitive grounds. Laudan also notes that the thesis of under-determination was held in various forms by Reichenbach, Hempel and Carnap. "Indeed," he writes, "a belief that underdetermination has profound ramifications for an understanding of the scientific enterprise is as positivist as a Viennese coffee house."[314]

In my view, the approach to causality proposed by thinkers such as Bhaskar, Harré and Madden and Ellis allows us to develop a parallel line of argument regarding the *ontological* ground of post-positivism. For a scientific essentialist, to use Ellis's term, post-positivist perspectivism is not simply the "end-game" of logical positivist epistemology, as Laudan puts it. It also fits – as does positivism – into a post-Lockean *ontological* universe, in which the concept of real essence has been replaced with that of nominal essence. As intimated in Chapter 3, I believe that the shift from the concept of real (albeit for Locke mechanistically construed) essence to nominal essence sets the stage for relativism and anti-realism in their contemporary forms. The trajectory is as follows: from the real, internal constitutions of things, we move to linguistic classifications of manifest properties. The suggestion that an object's manifest properties are in fact caused by its internal constitution then drops out. In its place, we get the idea that objects just *are* those of their features that we have seen fit to collect under a name. The next step is to observe (correctly, in my view) that there is no metaphysically fixed relationship between names and that to which they refer – that is, that meaning is internal to language. Given the prior supplanting of the concept of real essence by that of nominal essence, this otherwise unexceptional step leads – not necessarily, but nevertheless coherently – to precisely the rejection of a correspondence approach to the concept of truth and of metaphysical realism that characterize the post-positivist stance. Depending on whether one puts a Kantian, pragmatist or idealist spin on things, one then says that it is impossible to talk about what the world is like "in itself," that all claims are equally true because language is non-representational in the first place and/or that we really do engage in world-making, as Nelson Goodman puts it. The point, to reiterate, is not that there is a relationship of logical implication between each of these steps, but rather that, at the deepest level, the ontological terms of the debate are set by the move from real to nominal essences.

314 Laudan, *Beyond Positivism and Relativism: Theory, Method, and Evidence,* p. 20.

Locke himself emerges from such an analysis as a pivotal yet ambiguous figure. He appears to be ontologically committed to the existence of real essences, but to regard them as epistemologically moot. There is disagreement over whether Locke thinks that real essences are necessarily unknowable or only contingently so.[315] Even if the latter, however, Locke does not seem to hold out any hope that the situation will change: what knowledge we do and can expect to have is of the manifest properties of entities rather than of their inaccessible inner workings. Moreover, while Locke is committed to the existence of real essences, he conceives of nature in mechanistic terms. At the same time, as I believe Bhaskar, as well as Harré and Madden to have shown, Locke's notion of real essence can be used as the starting point for a non-Humean account of causal explanation.

It seems to me that the tensions in Locke's position are reflected in Bhaskar and Ellis's differing treatments of him. For Bhaskar, Locke is, while not the hero of the story, at least an ally. Bhaskar casts Locke in a basically positive light in relation to transcendental realism. He focuses on the importance of Locke's distinction between real and nominal essences, and seems to have no trouble combining Locke's notion of real essence with Leibniz's affirmation of causal powers in nature.[316] For Ellis, meanwhile, Locke is one of the villains of the piece. Ellis focuses on Locke's mechanism, and draws attention to the pronounced difference between Locke's views and those of Leibniz regarding whether or not matter is essentially inert. I don't think that there is any great need to adjudicate this difference of placement. What is crucial is the juncture in history of philosophy that Locke marks.

Ultimately, critical realism is significant because it points us in an unexpected direction. The implication of Bhaskar's work – and the explicit thesis of Ellis's – is that if we want to move beyond positivism, we must move beyond anti-essentialism. There is a certain irony to this conclusion, given the popular misidentification of positivism with essentialism. But logical positivism, as empiricism generally, is a thoroughly anti-essentialist philosophical stance, from the perspective of which ultimately contingent relationships between surface appearances are all that we can or should hope to know. Admittedly there have been objectionable versions of essentialism within Western philosophy. It is important to emphasize,

315 R. S. Woolhouse, *Locke's Philosophy of Science and Knowledge: A Consideration of Some Aspects of An Essay Concerning Human Understanding*, Oxford: Basil Blackwell, 1971, pp. 112–114.
316 Bhaskar, *RTS*, pp. 171–175.

therefore, that the essentialism that is being recommended – and the naturalism about causality to which it is connected – differs appreciably from earlier forms.

Scientific essentialism, to use Ellis's term again, is a relatively modest metaphysics. Its proponents do not invoke essences that can only be intuited, or that function as underlying intentional forces. Nor is there the suggestion that essences are inherently good, or that social life ought not to change or be changed (or, conversely, that it will develop necessarily in one way or another, in keeping with its essence). As described in Chapter 1, the fundamental claim is that things have intrinsic characteristics, which are necessarily connected to real powers. Such a claim may strike one as either banal or dangerous, depending upon one's predisposition. I hope to have shown that it is neither. Bhaskar (and others) have by no means resolved the philosophical problems associated with the concepts of truth and reality, but they have at least set out a viable alternative to positivism and post-positivism alike.

Bibliography

Adorno, Theodor W. (ed. Rolf Tiedemann, trans. Rodney Livingstone) *Kant's Critique of Pure Reason*, Stanford, CA: Stanford University Press, 2001.

Adorno, Theodor W. "Husserl and the Problem of Idealism," *The Journal of Philosophy*, 37(1), January 1940, 5–18.

Adorno, Theodor W. *Negative Dialectics*, New York: The Continuum Publishing Company, 1992.

Alcoff, Linda Martin *Real Knowing: New Versions of the Coherence Theory*, Ithaca, NY: Cornell University Press, 1996.

Allison, Henry E. *Kant's Transcendental Idealism: An Interpretation and Defense*, New Haven, CT: Yale University Press, 1983.

Alston, William P. *A Realist Conception of Truth*, Ithaca, NY: Cornell University Press, 1996.

Aristotle (trans. Robin Waterfield) *Physics*, Oxford: Oxford University Press, 1996.

Aristotle *Metaphysics*, in Richard McKeon (ed.), *The Basic Works of Aristotle*, New York: Random House, 1941.

Benton, Ted "Realism and Social Science: Some Comments on Roy Bhaskar's 'The Possibility of Naturalism,'" in Margaret Archer, Roy Bhaskar, Andrew Collier, Tony Lawson and Alan Norrie (eds), *Critical Realism: Essential Readings*, London: Routledge, 1998.

Bhaskar, Roy *A Realist Theory of Science*, Sussex: The Harvester Press Limited, 1978 (first published 1975).

Bhaskar, Roy *Scientific Realism and Human Emancipation*, London: Verso, 1986.

Bhaskar, Roy *Reclaiming Reality: A Critical Introduction to Contemporary Philosophy*, London: Verso, 1989.

Bhaskar, Roy *Dialectic: The Pulse of Freedom*, London: Verso, 1993.

Bhaskar, Roy *Plato, Etc.: The Problems of Philosophy and Their Resolution*, London: Verso, 1994.

Bhaskar, Roy *The Possibility of Naturalism: A Philosophical Critique of the Contemporary Human Sciences*, 3rd edn, London: Routledge, 1998.

Bhaskar, Roy and Lawson, Tony "Introduction: Basic Texts and Developments," in Margaret Archer, Roy Bhaskar, Andrew Collier, Tony Lawson and Alan Norrie (eds), *Critical Realism: Essential Readings*, London: Routledge, 1998.

Bigelow, John "Skeptical Realism: A Realist's Defense of Dummet," *The Monist*, 77(1), 1994, 3–26.

Brittan, George G., Jr *Kant's Theory of Science*, Princeton, NJ: Princeton University Press, 1978.

Chakravartty, Anjan "The Dispositional Essentialist View of Properties and Laws," forthcoming in *Philosophical Studies*, December 2003.

Collier, Andrew *Critical Realism: An Introduction to Roy Bhaskar's Philosophy*, London: Verso, 1994.

Collins, Arthur *Possible Experience: Understanding Kant's Critique of Pure Reason*, Berkeley: University of California Press, 1999.

Copi, Irving M. "Essence and Accident," in Stephen P. Schwartz (ed.), *Naming, Necessity and Natural Kinds*, Ithaca, NY: Cornell University Press, 1977.

Danermark, Berth, Ekstrom, Mats, Jakobsen, Losolette and Karlsson, Jan Ch. *Explaining Society: Critical Realism in the Social Sciences*, London: Routledge, 2002.

Davidson, Donald "The Folly of Trying to Define Truth," *The Journal of Philosophy*, 93(6), June 1996, 263–278.

Davidson, Donald "Truth Rehabilitated," in Robert B. Brandom (ed.), *Rorty and his Critics*, Malden, MA: Blackwell Publishers, 2000.

Devitt, Michael *Realism and Truth*, 2nd edn, Princeton, NJ: Princeton University Press, 1991.

Dreyfus, Hubert L. "Heidegger's Hermeneutic Realism," in David R. Hiley, James F. Bohman and Richard Schusterman (eds), *The Interpretive Turn: Philosophy, Science, Culture*, Ithaca, NY: Cornell University Press, 1991.

Eagleton, Terry *The Illusions of Postmodernism*, Oxford: Blackwell Publishers, 1996.

Ellis, Brian "Causal Powers and Laws of Nature," in Howard Sankey (ed.), *Causation and Laws of Nature*, London: Kluwer Academic Publishers, 1999.

Ellis, Brian "Bigelow's Worries about Scientific Essentialism," in Howard Sankey (ed.), *Causation and Laws of Nature*, London: Kluwer Academic Publishers, 1999.

Ellis, Brian *Scientific Essentialism*, Cambridge: Cambridge University Press, 2001.

Flax, Jane "The End of Innocence," in Judith Butler and Joan W. Scott (eds), *Feminists Theorize the Political*, London: Routledge, 1992.

French, Peter A., Uehling, Theodore E., Jr and Wettstein, Howard K. (eds) *Midwest Studies in Philosophy, Vol. 9: Causation and Causal Theories*, Minneapolis: University of Minnesota Press, 1984.

Fukuyama, F. *Trust: The Social Virtues and the Creation of Prosperity*, London: Hamish Hamilton, 1995.

Garcia-Encinas, M. J. "Sullivan on the Principle that Everything Has a Cause," *Dialogue: Canadian Philosophical Review*, XLI(3), Summer 2002.

Geertz, Clifford "The Strange Estrangement: Taylor and the Natural Sciences," in James Tully (ed.), *Philosophy in an Age of Pluralism: The Philosophy of Charles Taylor in Question*, Cambridge: Cambridge University Press, 1994.

Gibson-Graham, J. K. "Waiting for the Revolution, or How to Smash Capitalism While Working at Home in Your Spare Time," in Antonio Callari, Stephen Cullenberg and Carole Biewener (eds), *Marxism in the Postmodern Age: Confronting the New World Order*, New York: The Guilford Press, 1995.

Green, J. Everet *Kant's Copernican Revolution: The Transcendental Horizon*, Lanham, MD: University Press of America, 1997.

Groff, Ruth "Reason Reconsidered: Political Education, Critical Theory and the Concept of Rational Critique," unpublished MA thesis, University of Toronto, 1994.

Guignon, Charles B. "Pragmatism or Hermeneutics? Epistemology After Foundationalism," in David R. Hiley, James F. Bohman and Richard Schusterman (eds), *The Interpretive Turn: Philosophy, Science, Culture*, Ithaca, NY: Cornell University Press, 1991.

Hacking, Ian *Representing and Intervening: Introductory Topics in the Philosophy of Natural Science*, Cambridge: Cambridge University Press, 1983.

Harré, Rom and Bhaskar, Roy "How To Change Reality: Story vs. Structure: A Debate Between Rom Harré and Roy Bhaskar," in Jose Lopez and Garry Potter (eds.), *After Postmodernism: An Introduction to Critical Realism*, London: The Athlone Press, 2001.

Harré, Rom and Madden, E. H. *Causal Powers: A Theory of Natural Necessity*, Totowa, NY: Rowman and Littlefield, 1975.

Horkheimer, Max *Critical Theory: Selected Essays*, New York: The Continuum Publishing Corporation, 1989.

Hume, David (ed. Anthony Flew) *On Human Nature and the Understanding*, New York: Collier Books, 1962.

Hutton, W. *The State We're In*, London: Vintage Books, 1996.

Jarvis, Simon *Adorno: A Critical Introduction*, New York: Routledge, 1998.

Jolley, Nicholas *Leibniz and Locke: A Study of the New Essays on Human Understanding*, Oxford: Clarendon Press, 1984.

Jones, W. T. *A History of Western Philosophy: Kant and the Nineteenth Century*, 2nd edn, revised, New York: Harcourt Brace Jovanovich, 1975.

Kant, Immanuel (trans. Paul Carus) *Prolegomena to any Future Metaphysics that can Qualify as a Science*, La Salle, IL: Open Court Publishing Company, 1902, 6th printing, 1988.

Kant, Immanuel (trans. and ed. Paul Guyer and Allen W. Wood) *Critique of Pure Reason*, New York: Cambridge University Press, 1997.

Kirk, Robert, *Relativism and Reality: A Contemporary Introduction*, London: Routledge, 1999.

Kirkham, Richard L. *Theories of Truth: A Critical Introduction*, Cambridge, MA: MIT Press, 1995.

Kuhn, Thomas S. *The Structure of Scientific Revolutions*, 2nd edn, enlarged, Chicago: The University of Chicago Press, 1970.

Kuhn, Thomas S. "The Natural and the Human Sciences," in David R. Hiley, James F. Bohman and Richard Schusterman (eds), *The Interpretive Turn: Philosophy, Science, Culture*, Ithaca, NY: Cornell University Press, 1991.

Laudan, Larry *Beyond Positivism and Relativism: Theory, Method, and Evidence* , Boulder, CO: Westview Press, 1996.

Lear, Jonathan *Aristotle: The Desire To Understand*, Cambridge: Cambridge University Press, 1988.

Lewis, Paul "Realism, Causality and the Problem of Social Structure," *Journal for the Theory of Social Behavior*, 30(3), September 2000.

Locke, John *An Essay Concerning Human Understanding* (abridged and with Notes by A. S. Pringle-Pattison), Hertfordshire: Wordsworth Editions Limited, 1998.

McDermid, Douglas "Pragmatism and Truth: The Comparison Objection to Correspondence," *The Review of Metaphysics*, 51, June 1998.

McDowell, John "Towards Rehabilitating Objectivity," in Robert B. Brandom (ed.), *Rorty and his Critics*, Malden, MA: Blackwell Publishers, 2000.

MacIntyre, Alasdair "Emotion, Behavior and Belief," and "Is a Science of Comparative Politics Possible?" in *Against the Self-Images of the Age: Essays on Ideology and Philosophy*, Notre Dame, IN: University of Notre Dame Press, 1978.

MacIntyre, Alasdair *After Virtue: A Study in Moral Theory*, Notre Dame, IN: University of Notre Dame Press, 1981.

MacIntyre, Alasdair "Relativism, Power, and Philosophy," in Kenneth Baynes, James Bohman and Thomas McCarthy (eds), *After Philosophy: End or Transformation?*, Cambridge, MA: MIT Press, 1987.

Norris, Christopher, "Truth, Science and the Growth of Knowledge: On the Limits of Cultural Relativism," in *Reclaiming Truth: Contributions to a Critique of Cultural Relativism*, Durham, NC: Duke University Press, 1996.

Norris, Christopher "Hermeneutics, Anti-realism and Philosophy of Science," in *Against Relativism: Philosophy of Science, Deconstruction and Critical Theory*, Oxford: Blackwell Publishers, 1997.

Norris, Christopher "Putnam's Progress: Quantum Theory and the Flight from Realism," *The Philosophical Forum*, 30(2), June 1999, 61–90.

Outhwaite, William "Realism and Social Science," in Margaret Archer, Roy Bhaskarm Andrew Collier, Tony Lawson and Alan Norrie (eds), *Critical Realism: Essential Readings*, London: Routledge, 1998.

Popper, Sir Karl (ed. W. W. Bartley III), *Realism and the Aim of Science: From the Postscript to the Logic of Scientific Discovery*, New York: Routledge, 1983.

Popper, Sir Karl *Conjectures and Refutations: The Growth of Scientific Knowledge*, New York: Routledge, 1989.

Porpora, Douglas *The Concept of Social Structure*, Westport, CT: Greenwood Press, 1987.

Porpora, Douglas "Four Concepts of Social Structure," in Margaret Archer, Roy Bhaskar, Andrew Collier, Tony Lawson and Alan Norrie (eds), *Critical Realism: Essential Readings*, London: Routledge, 1998.

Putnam, Hilary *Reason, Truth and History*, Cambridge: Cambridge University Press, 1981.

Putnam, Hilary "Why Reason Can't be Naturalized," in Kenneth Baynes, James Bohman and Thomas McCarthy (eds), *After Philosophy: End or Transformation?*, Cambridge, MA: MIT Press, 1987.

Putnam, Hilary (ed. James Conant) *Realism with a Human Face*, Cambridge, MA: Harvard University Press, 1990.

Putnam, Hilary *Renewing Philosophy*, Cambridge, MA: Harvard University Press, 1992.

Putnam, Hilary "Is There Still Anything to Say about Reality and Truth?" in Peter J. McCormick (ed.) *Starmaking: Realism, Anti-Realism and Irrealism*, Cambridge, MA: MIT Press, 1996.

Putnam, Hilary "Irrealism and Deconstruction" in Peter J. McCormick (ed.) *Starmaking: Realism, Anti-Realism and Irrealism*, Cambridge, MA: MIT Press, 1996.

Putnam, Hilary *The Threefold Cord: Mind, Body and the World (The John Dewey Essays in Philosophy, Number 5)*, New York: Columbia University Press, 1999.

Putnam, Hilary "Richard Rorty on Reality and Justification," in Robert B. Brandom (ed.), *Rorty and his Critics*, Malden, MA: Blackwell Publishers, 2000.

Rescher, Nicholas *Kant's Theory of Knowledge and Reality: A Group of Essays*, Washington, DC: University Presss of America, 1983.

Rorty, Richard *Objectivity, Relativism and Truth: Philosophical Papers*, vol. 1, Cambridge: Cambridge University Press, 1991.

Rorty, Richard *Truth and Progress: Philosohical Papers*, vol. 3, New York: Cambridge University Press, 1998.

Rorty, Richard *Philosophy and Social Hope*, Harmondsworth: Penguin Books, 1999.

Rouse, Joseph "Interpretation in Natural and Human Science," in David R. Hiley, James F. Bohman and Richard Schusterman (eds), *The Interpretive Turn: Philosophy, Science, Culture*, Ithaca, NY: Cornell University Press, 1991.

Schmitt, Frederick *Truth: A Primer*, Boulder, CO: Westview Press, 1995.

Schrag, Calvin O. *The Resources of Rationality: A Response to the Postmodern Challenge*, Bloomington: Indiana University Press, 1992.

Taylor, Charles *The Explanation of Behavior*, London and Henley: Routledge & Kegan Paul, 1964.

Taylor, Charles *Human Agency and Language: Philosophical Papers 1*, Cambridge: Cambridge University Press, 1985.

Taylor, Charles *Philosophy and the Human Sciences: Philosophical Papers 2*, Cambridge: Cambridge University Press, 1985.

Taylor, Charles "Overcoming Epistemology," in Kenneth Baynes, James Bohman and Thomas McCarthy (eds), *After Philosophy: End or Transformation?*, Cambridge, MA: MIT Press, 1987.

Taylor, Charles "Rorty in the Epistemological Tradition," in Alan R. Malachowski (ed.), *Reading Rorty: Critical Responses to Philosophy and the Mirror of Nature (and Beyond)*, Oxford: Basil Blackwell, 1990.

Taylor, Charles "Charles Taylor Replies," in James Tully (ed.), *Philosophy in an Age of Pluralism: The Philosophy of Charles Taylor in Question*, Cambridge: Cambridge University Press, 1994.

Taylor, Charles *Philosophical Explanations*, Cambridge, MA: Harvard University Press, 1995.

Varela, Charles R. "The Ethogenics of Agency and Structure: A Metaphysical Problem," in Jose Lopez and Garry Potter (eds), *After Postmodernism: An Introduction to Critical Realism*, London: The Athlone Press, 2001.

Varela, Charles R. "The Impossibility of Which Naturalism? A Response and Reply," *Journal for the Theory of Social Behavior*, 32(1), March 2002.

Varela, Charles R. and Harré, Rom "Conflicting Varieties of Realism: Causal Powers and the Problems of Social Structure," *Journal for the Theory of Social Behavior*, 26(3), 1986.

Woolhouse, R. S. *Locke's Philosophy of Science and Knowledge: A Consideration of Some Aspects of An Essay Concerning Human Understanding*, Oxford: Basil Blackwell, 1971.

Index